THE PROPHETIC INTERCESSION PRAYER GUIDE

HEARING GOD'S VOICE TO PRAY HEAVEN ON EARTH

ROMA WATERMAN

TABLE OF CONTENTS

PART II
THE INTERCESSOR'S TOOLKIT: UNLOCKING DIVINE COMMUNICATION

PART III
DIVING DEEPER: DEEPENING THE PRACTICE

FOREWORD BY
Rosalia Balassone

*I*ntercession. It is the privilege of working with God. Being a shareholder in what God is doing. It is investing in Him. To experience Him at new levels of love.

I find it my greatest treasure and pleasure to join with His heart's desire as I yield and *blend* with Him to partner with Him in His pursuits. He loves people and nations and so must we, and He pours that love into and through us.

For you, dear reader, let us meet at God's throne. In Roma's book, *Prophetic Intercession*, you will find marvelous guidelines to encourage you in your journey, both from Scripture and from other experienced intercessors. The nuggets of wisdom you find in its pages will add to what you already hold in your heart.

This book carries a weight and anointing. I have learnt so much from reading it, and I know you will be blessed with this aid for His glory.

The heart of God is thrilled to have us join Him in His quests!

Rosalia Balassone

(Intercessor, mother of the author)

PREFACE BY
Roma Waterman

The school bell rings, signaling the end of the school day. As my siblings and I pile into the car, Mum greets us with a warm smile, our baby brother already secured in his seat.

After some afternoon tea, most days mum would say, "Right, I'm going to my room to pray; no one bother me and no fighting!" With that, she would walk up the stairs to the main bedroom, shut the door . . . and be gone for a couple of hours.

In one corner of her bedroom was a small wooden table, with her well-worn Bible always open, an array of pens, notebooks filled with scriptures and prayer requests, and the latest book she was reading. Not that we saw it much, because she would close the door and pray as if her life depended on it. It might as well have been a portal to another realm.

As we grew into teenage years, many sibling quarrels would arise during those hours between afternoon tea and dinner. Off one of us kids would march, pounding up the stairs yelling, "Mum! Mum!! Chris ate the last biscuit!!!" or "Mum, Mum, Damian said a swear word!" As I approached her closed door in my "righteous" anger, I would hear her speaking in tongues, praying fervently, and like a true Italian matriarch, she would only pause to shout, "Don't you dare open that door! I'm praying. Sort it out between yourselves!"

I have many memories of the powerful prayers my mum prayed. I recall us all in the car, dad ready to drive off on a family holiday down to the beach, yelling at mum who was still in the house and impatiently honking the horn. "Come on, mum, it's time to go! What is taking you so long?" we would all shout out the window alerting the whole street of our impatience. Mum was of course, going through every room of the house praying that angels would protect our home while we were not there. Once, as she locked the front door after a simple prayer, she gazed up the stairs in awe, for through the entrance window she witnessed several large angels descending into our living room and kitchen.

Another vivid memory: mum driving me to school, her face contorted with pain. Mum had a Bible in every room of the house, including the car. As we traveled down the main road, her face revealing the pain gripping her body, she said out loud, "Right that's it!" and promptly pulled over to the side of the road, pulled out her Bible and started quoting Isaiah 53: "By His stripes I am healed!!!" Moments later, all pain left her body and she resumed our journey as if nothing had happened. She fully expected that if she prayed, she would receive an answer.

This is how I remember my mum. The ultimate intercessor. Her prayers constantly covered us, our family, our church, and our school like a spiritual blanket of protection and blessing. I truly believe my calling into ministry today is a direct result of her petitions. Her consistent passion over decades has ignited my own fervor for prayer, a legacy I hope passes on to my own children, embedding intercession into the very fabric of our family tradition.

It's this passion that fuels "The Prophetic Intercession Prayer Guide." As you turn these pages, my deepest hope is that you'll be inspired to pray with the same intensity and expectation that characterized my mother's devotion. May you, too, learn to pray in a way that brings Heaven down to Earth, transforming lives and leaving an indelible mark on generations to come. God knows we need it.

Thanks mum, now it's my turn . . . I won't forget what you taught me.

Roma

INTRODUCTION:
How to Use This Prayer Guide

Welcome to the journey of deepening your practice of prophetic intercession. I am so glad you are here! Loving Jesus and hearing His voice is one of the greatest honors we can have as we serve Him in our time here on earth, and I pray this resource will inspire and encourage you to make prayer a priority.

This guide is designed to be a practical tool to help you grow in this powerful form of prayer. I wanted to create an easy-to-read, quick resource that would help activate people effectively in prophetic intercession, and I pray this will motivate you to go deeper in prayer, in the Word, and in your walk with the Lord.

It is meant to be used as a reference guide that can be part of your resource arsenal for prophetic intercession and prayer. I want to also encourage you to read the books I have used in my research and that are on the recommended reading list to extend your knowledge and understanding of prayer.

In each chapter you will find easy to reference scriptures, stories, thoughts and quotes. There is also a "prophetic intercession map" if you are new to prayer. This map is not a "rule" but may help you as a tool as you grow in prayer and prophetic intercession. If you are new to prayer or need a system, you may find this breakdown of how prayer can look helpful:

- Enter God's Presence
- Listen for God's Voice
- Discern the Message
- Reflect and Apply (if personal) / Intercede (if for others)
- Declare God's Will
- Wait on God
- Discern Further Guidance
- Give Thanks and Praise
- Act on Guidance
- Record and Share
- Evaluate and Learn

This map is not meant to be a rigid formula, but rather a flexible guide to help you navigate the flow of prophetic intercession. You may find yourself moving back and forth between steps or spending more time on certain aspects depending on God's leading. I also highly recommend reading the books in the bibliography that are comprehensive and some of my personal favorites.

How to Use This Guide:

1. **Start with the introduction:** Begin by reading the introductory chapter **What is Prophetic Intercession?** This will give you a solid foundation and historical context for the practice.

2. **Study each chapter:** Read the explanations, meditate on the scriptures provided, and, if the chapter has them, use the reflection questions to help you unpack what you are sensing and feeling.

3. **Try out the prompts:** Most chapters include practical suggestions of how to implement specific prayer themes and points. Don't rush through these—they are designed to help you apply what you are learning. Take time

to practice and experience each aspect of prophetic intercession and make it fun!

4. **Reflect and journal:** To deepen your understanding, journal your thoughts, experiences, and any insights you receive. This record will be valuable for tracking your growth, and the results of your prayers, over time. Date everything—it will become such an encouragement to you.

5. **Group study:** While this workbook can be used individually, it's also great for group study. Consider going through it with a prayer partner or small group, sharing insights and experiences.

6. **Revisit and review:** Don't feel pressured to complete the workbook in one go. Take your time, and feel free to revisit sections as needed. Prophetic intercession is a lifelong journey of growth!

7. **Practice regularly:** Set aside dedicated time to practice prophetic intercession using the principles learned. Consistency is key to growth in this area. Make it a lifestyle and it will change your life!

8. **Further study:** Utilize the books mentioned in the bibliography for deeper exploration of topics that particularly interest you.

Tips for Your Journey

- **Stay humble:** Remember, intercession is about partnering with God, not about personal power or influence.

- **Be patient:** Growing in intercession takes time. Don't be discouraged if you don't see immediate results.

- **Stay grounded in Scripture:** Always test prophetic impressions against the Word of God.

- **Community is key:** Share your journey with trusted believers who can offer support, accountability, and confirmation.

- **Embrace the learning process:** View challenges or mistakes as opportunities for growth and learning.

May this guide be a valuable tool in your journey with the Lord, helping you partner more closely with God in prayer and intercession. As you begin, take a moment to pray, inviting the Holy Spirit to guide you through this process of learning and growth.

A Prayer as We Begin This Journey

Heavenly Father,
Thank you for the gift of being able to
partner with You to bring Heaven to Earth.
Open my spiritual eyes to see beyond the
natural, and tune my ears to hear Your
voice with crystal clarity.

I thank You for the precious gift of prayer.
As I dive into these pages, I ask for the fresh
breath of Your Holy Spirit to flow through
and in me. Let Your words of life leap off
these pages and into my heart with new
revelation, power, and insight!

I pray that this book would be a tool I can
use to bring me closer to you. I prophesy
that lives will be transformed, bodies will be
healed, and Your Kingdom will advance as I
learn to partner with You in prayer.

Stir up the gifts within me, Lord! Let words
of prophecy flow like rivers of living water.
May my intercession shake the heavens and
change the earth!

I pray that every chain of confusion or complacency would be broken right now by the power of Jesus' name. I am stepping into a new season of power, purpose, and prophetic precision!

With excitement and anticipation, I say YES to all You have for me in this journey.

In the mighty name of Jesus I pray,

Amen!

Part I

LAYING THE GROUNDWORK: THE ROOTS AND RHYTHMS OF PROPHETIC INTERCESSION

CHAPTER 1

WHAT IS PROPHETIC INTERCESSION?

*P*rophetic intercession is a powerful fusion of two spiritual practices: prophecy and intercessory prayer. It's a divine partnership where the intercessor seeks God's heart and mind concerning a person, situation, or place, and then prays according to God's revealed will. This form of prayer goes beyond our limited understanding, tapping into God's infinite wisdom and perspective.

Intercession is different than normal prayer; it is a way to pray that "pushes through" and contends for what one senses is on the Lord's heart. I like the way Joseph Z says it:

> *Intercession* is—allowing the Holy Spirit to *pray through you* coupled with prophecy, which in this instance would be to see and

"say" what the Lord is speaking. Tactically, this combination releases sharp, effective prayers with weaponized accuracy that can strike any target with maximum results. God needs your prayers; without them, His will won't automatically come to pass.[1]

In his book, *The Prophetic Intercessor*, James Goll describes prophetic intercession as "an urge to pray, given by the Holy Spirit, for a situation or circumstance about which you may have little natural knowledge. But you are praying the prayer request that is on the heart of God."[2]

He goes on to explain that prophetic intercession is praying God's heart back to Him, as He imparts His burden to you. This kind of prayer requires waiting, listening, going deep in the scriptures, and drawing closer to the Lord so we can be confident in hearing and knowing His voice.

What Makes Prayer Prophetic?

We might pray because we have a desire or a request from God, but the prophetic component of prayer is when a person hears the desire or longing from the

---

[1] Joseph Z, *Servants of Fire* (Shippensburg, PA: Harrison House, 2023), 20.

[2] James W. Goll, *The Prophetic Intercessor: Releasing God's Purposes to Change Lives and Influence Nations* (Grand Rapids, MI: Chosen Books, 2007), 145–46.

heart of God, and prays from that place. I love this passage in Jeremiah:

> If they are prophets, and if the word of the LORD is with them, let them now entreat the LORD of hosts. (Jer. 27:18, NASB1995)

Jeremiah was presenting the false prophets in this passage with a challenge—if they were truly prophets of God, they should be able to intercede with God on behalf of the people. But Jeremiah understood that it required the word of the Lord, His voice, and His desire to pray. He knew they didn't have this and that their prayers would not be effective. Prophetic intercession is the word of the Lord in your prayer, and as you carry His heart, you can pray His promise! You "entreat" as this passage says, the Lord of Hosts. To entreat means to ask someone sincerely and urgently for something or to plead with someone.

While prayer itself is a powerful spiritual discipline, what distinguishes prophetic intercession is the intercessor's ability to discern and align with God's heart. This form of prayer is not simply presenting requests to God, but rather positioning oneself to hear God's desires and intentions for a situation, person, or nation. The prophetic intercessor becomes a conduit for God's voice, not just speaking to God on behalf of others, but also speaking God's words back to Him and to the world. This dynamic interaction requires a deep sensitivity to the Holy Spirit, an understanding of God's character as revealed in Scripture, and a willingness to stand in the gap between heaven and earth.

In essence, prophetic intercession is less about informing God of needs (which He already knows) and more about partnering with Him to bring His kingdom purposes to fruition through prayer that is informed by divine insight and revelation.

Biblical Foundations

The concept of prophetic intercession is rooted in Scripture. The prophet Amos declared:

Surely the Sovereign LORD does nothing without revealing his plan to his servants the prophets. (Amos 3:7)

This verse suggests that God desires to communicate His plans to His people. In the context of intercession, it implies that God wants to guide our prayers, aligning them with His will.

The apostle John refers to this same truth in his Gospel, when he records the words of Jesus on the night before He died:

> I have much more to say to you, more than you can now bear. But when he, the Spirit of truth, comes, he will guide you into all the truth. He will not speak on his own; he will speak only what he hears, and he will tell you what is yet to come. He will glorify me because it is from me that he will receive what he will make known to you. All that belongs to the Father is mine. That is why I said the Spirit will receive from me what he will make known to you. (John 16:12–15)

We see from Scripture that the Holy Spirit aids us in our prayers, especially when the whole truth surpasses us. Little by little He teaches us how to pray and makes known to us what is yet to come. This Heavenly assistance is at the heart of prophetic intercession.

Unpacking Prophetic Intercession

1. **Listening prayer**: At its core, prophetic intercession begins with listening. To quote

James Goll again, when discussing the importance of listening in prayer, he says:

In order to cultivate a spirit of revelation—the prophetic presence of God in our lives there is another key for us to use. The fast-paced, instant society of our day is diametrically opposed to the gentle, quiet spirits we need to be people of revelation. The Holy Spirit is searching eagerly for those on whose quiet hearts He can write the revelatory words of God.[3]

Listening prayer involves cultivating a sensitivity to God's voice and being willing to pray beyond our own understanding or agenda.

2. **Praying God's will**: Jesus taught His disciples to pray, "Your kingdom come, Your will be done, on earth as it is in heaven" (Matt. 6:10). Prophetic intercessors seek to discern God's will and pray it into existence.

3. **Spiritual warfare:** Often, prophetic intercession involves engaging in spiritual warfare. As the prophet Daniel experienced (Dan. 10:12–13), there can be spiritual resistance to God's plans, requiring persistent, informed prayer.

---

[3] Goll, *The Prophetic Intercessor*, 86.

4. **Declaration and proclamation**: Prophetic intercessors often find themselves declaring God's promises and proclaiming His truth over situations. This aligns with God's word to Jeremiah: "See, today I appoint you over nations and kingdoms to uproot and tear down, to destroy and overthrow, to build and to plant" (Jer. 1:10).

5. **Burden bearing:** Prophetic intercessors often carry a deep burden for what they are praying about. Norman Grubb in his biography of intercessor Rees Howells shares a story that reflects this poignantly:

He was called in to see a man in the village who was dying. He found him already unconscious. His wife was sobbing her heart out, for there were ten children, and he was the only bread-winner. The effect on Mr. Howells was immediate. The suffering of the woman came to him as if it were his own sister. He went out into a field and wept and, as he said, "Once you weep, or the Holy Ghost in you, you are the very one to touch the Throne."[4]

---

[4] Norman P. Grubb, *Rees Howells: Intercessor* (Fort Washington, PA: Christian Literature Crusade, 1971), 96.

Historical Examples

Throughout history, we see examples of prophetic intercession at work:

- **Abraham**: In Genesis 18, Abraham intercedes for Sodom after God reveals His plans. God changes what He will do based on Abraham's intervention (or prayer). This demonstrates how God invites His people into His decision-making process through prayer.

- **Moses:** Exodus 32 and Numbers 14 show Moses interceding for Israel after God reveals His intention to destroy them. Moses' prayer, based on God's character and promises, led to a change in the situation.

- **Anna:** In Luke 2:36–38, we meet Anna, a prophetess who "never left the temple but worshiped night and day, fasting and praying." Her life of devotion positioned her to recognize Jesus as the long-awaited Messiah.

Modern-Day Impact: The Remarkable Story of Rees Howells

In more recent times, we've seen the power of prophetic intercession through stories like that of

Rees Howells (1879–1950), a Welsh coal miner turned intercessor and missionary.[5]

In 1924, Howells founded the Bible College of Wales, which became a center for intercessory prayer. The college's primary purpose was not just education, but intercession for world events guided by prophetic insights. In World War II, Howells led a group of intercessors and, through prophetic insights, they prayed strategically at critical moments of the war, witnessing remarkable answers to prayer that aligned with key turning points in the conflict.

EARLY LIFE AND CALLING

Rees Howells was born in a small mining village in Wales. At the age of 23, during the Welsh Revival of 1904–1905, Howells experienced a profound encounter with God that changed the course of his life. He felt called to a life of full-time intercession, a concept that was radical for his time.

THE SCHOOL OF PRAYER

Howells described his early years in ministry as a "school of prayer." He learned to listen intently to God's voice and to pray with remarkable specificity. Biographer Norman Grubb recounts that Rees Howells' intercessory prayer life was characterized

---

[5] Grubb, *Rees Howells: Intercessor.*

by receiving clear directives from God, often accompanied by prophetic insights into future events or hidden realities.

This aligns closely with our understanding of prophetic intercession—praying not just from human understanding, but from divine revelation.

WORLD WAR II INTERCESSION

The most dramatic example of Howells' prophetic intercession came during World War II. Howells and his team at the Bible College of Wales engaged in intense, focused prayer throughout the war, guided by what they believed were prophetic insights from God.

Norman Grubb, in his biography, wrote how, time and again, Rees Howells received what he believed to be prophetic insights into the course of the war, which guided the intercessions of the entire college. The alignment between these prayers and subsequent events was remarkable on many occasions. Some notable instances include:

1. **Dunkirk Evacuation**: In May 1940, when over 335,000 Allied troops were trapped at Dunkirk, Howells and his team prayed for their miraculous evacuation. The successful

operation, often called the "Miracle of Dunkirk," aligned with their prayers.

2. **Battle of Britain:** During the critical air battles over Britain in 1940, Howells and his intercessors prayed specifically for the protection of Britain from invasion. Despite being vastly outnumbered, the Royal Air Force prevailed, and the planned Nazi invasion was postponed indefinitely.

3. **El Alamein:** Before the decisive battle of El Alamein in 1942, Howells received what he believed was a prophetic word that this battle would mark the turning point of the war in North Africa. The Allied victory indeed proved to be a crucial turning point.

4. **D-Day:** As the Allied forces prepared for the Normandy invasion, Howells and his team prayed intensely for its success, claiming to have received assurance from God about the operation's outcome.

Rees Howells' approach to prophetic intercession left a lasting impact on the Christian understanding of prayer. His life demonstrated the key principles of prophetic intercession that we mentioned earlier in this chapter:

1. **Listening prayer:** Howells emphasized the importance of hearing from God before praying, aligning human prayers with divine will.

2. **Specificity in prayer:** His intercessions were often remarkably specific, guided by what he believed were prophetic insights.

3. **Persistence:** Howells and his team would often pray for extended periods, sometimes months or years, for a single issue.

4. **Faith and boldness:** Howells prayed with great faith, often making bold declarations based on what he believed God had revealed.

5. **Community intercession:** While Howells had a unique calling, he emphasized the power of united, corporate prayer.

Doris Ruscoe, a student at the Bible College of Wales during the war years, later compared the events of those years to the "strange plot" found in Judges 20:

> Twice the men of Judah asked counsel of God and went up against Benjamin, only to be driven back each time with great slaughter. But after a national day of prayer and fasting the word of assurance was given and victory came on the third attempt. So throughout those years,

in a real war situation, the Word of God came alive to us in a new way and daily the Holy Spirit sustained us as we fought on, knowing that the real battle was in the heavenlies, and over and over again seeing the outcome of a spiritual victory demonstrated later in the actual fighting.[6]

The story of Rees Howells provides a powerful, real-world example of prophetic intercession in action. It illustrates how this form of prayer can potentially impact not just individual lives, but world events. Howells' life stands as a testament to the potential power of prayer guided by prophetic insight.

Other Notable Examples of Prophetic Intercessors

While Rees Howells provides a compelling example of prophetic intercession, he is far from the only figure known for this practice. Here are a few other notable individuals:

1. **Dutch Sheets:** Author and teacher, Sheets is known for his teachings on prophetic intercession and strategic prayer. His approach involves seeking God for specific insights to

---

6 Doris M. Ruscoe, *The Intercession of Rees Howells, 1879–1950* (Fort Washington, PA: Christian Literature Crusade, 1983), 25.

guide prayer efforts for cities, nations, and global issues.

2. **Cindy Jacobs:** Prophet and Co-founder of Generals International, Jacobs is recognized for her prophetic ministry and her teaching on prayer and intercession. She often leads large-scale prayer initiatives based on prophetic insights for nations and global events.

3. **Lou Engle:** Founder of The Call prayer movement, Engle has mobilized millions in fasting and prayer. His ministry frequently involves prophetic acts of intercession, often focused on cultural issues and spiritual awakening.

4. **Elizabeth Alves:** A pioneer in the modern prayer movement, Alves has taught extensively on prophetic intercession, emphasizing the importance of listening prayer and praying God's purposes.

5. **James W. Goll:** Goll has written extensively on prophetic intercession, combining biblical teaching with practical application.

These modern-day intercessors demonstrate various approaches to prophetic intercession, from personal prayer practices to large-scale prayer movements, all guided by what they believe to be prophetic insights.

Conclusion

Prophetic intercession is a powerful way to pray that bridges the gap between God's perfect will and earthly realities. It requires humility, sensitivity to the Holy Spirit, and a willingness to partner with God in bringing His kingdom to earth. As we delve deeper into the practices of prophetic intercession, may we approach it with reverence, expectation, and a deep desire to see God's purposes fulfilled in our world.

CHAPTER 2

VOICES THROUGH TIME: PROPHETIC INTERCESSION IN CHURCH HISTORY

Introduction

Prophetic intercession, while sometimes considered a modern charismatic practice, is so much more, and has deep roots in church history. From the early church to the present day, believers have engaged in prayer that combines deep intimacy with God, prophetic insight, and fervent intercession. As we explore this rich history, we see the fulfillment of Joel's prophecy, quoted by Peter in Acts 2:17: "In the last days, God says, I will pour out my Spirit on all people. Your sons and daughters will prophesy . . ." Let's take a brief look at what intercession has looked like over the course of time.

Early Church (1st-3rd c.)

The early church was marked by a strong emphasis on prayer and prophetic gifts. The book of Acts provides numerous examples of prophetic intercession in action. For example, Acts 13:1–3 describes the church at Antioch fasting and praying when the Holy Spirit spoke, directing them to send out Barnabas and Saul for missionary work.

Tertullian (AD 155–240), an early Christian author, wrote about the continuing practice of prophecy in the church. In his work *A Treatise on the Soul*, he describes how during worship services, a member of their worshipping community would sometimes fall into ecstatic states and deliver prophetic messages, often including calls to prayer for specific situations.[7]

Medieval Period (4th-15th c.)

During this period, prophetic intercession often manifested within monastic communities and through Christian mystics who reported visions and divine communications.

Hildegard of Bingen (1098–1179) for example, a Benedictine abbess, experienced visions which

---

[7] Tertullian, *A Treatise on the Soul* 9, in *Ante-Nicene Fathers*, vol. 3, *Latin Christianity*, ed. Alexander Roberts and James Donaldson (New York, Christian Literature Publishing, 1885).

she believed were divine revelations. These visions often led her to intercede for the church and society. In her book *Scivias*, she records prophetic insights that guided her prayers for reform in the church.[8]

Catherine of Siena (1347–1380), a lay consecrated woman, was known for her mystical experiences and intercessory prayer. Many of her letters contained prophetic insights that bear witness to her passionate intercession for the church and political leaders of her time.[9]

Reformation and Post-Reformation Era (16th–18th c.)

The Protestant Reformation brought renewed emphasis on personal prayer and direct communication with God.

George Fox (1624–1691), founder of the Quakers, emphasized the "Inner Light" or direct revelation from God. This often manifested in what we might call prophetic intercession. In his journal, Fox records instances of being led by the Spirit to pray

---

[8] Hildegard of Bingen, *Scivias*, trans. Mother Columba Hart and Jane Bishop (Mahwah, NJ: Paulist Press, 1990).

[9] Catherine of Siena, *The Letters of Catherine of Siena*, trans. Suzanne Noffke (Temple, AZ: Arizona Center for Medieval and Renaissance Studies, 2000).

for specific situations and individuals, often with remarkable results.[10]

John Knox (1513–1572), the Scottish Reformer, was known for his powerful intercessory prayer. Mary, Queen of Scots, is reported to have said, "I fear the prayers of John Knox more than all the assembled armies of Europe."[11]

Modern Era (19th–21st c.)

The modern era has seen a resurgence of interest in prophetic gifts and intercessory prayer movements.

You will notice that I mention Rees Howells (1879–1950) several times through this book, as a powerful example of someone who devoted their life to intercession. Howells developed a ministry of intercessory prayer that he believed was often guided by prophetic insights. During World War II, Howells and his team at the Bible College of Wales engaged in focused intercession for world events, claiming to receive specific guidance from God that shaped their prayers.[12]

---

[10] George Fox, *The Journal of George Fox,* ed. John L. Nickalls (Philadelphia: Philadelphia Yearly Meeting of the Religious Society of Friends, 1997).

[11] Brian G. Najapfour, "'Give me Scotland, or I die': John Knox as a Man of Prayer," *The Heritage Blog,* accessed September 12, 2024, https://www.theheritage.blog/knox-man-of-prayer.

[12] Grubb, *Rees Howells: Intercessor.*

Other notable figures include Smith Wigglesworth who has often been quoted as saying "I never pray for more than fifteen minutes at a time, but I never go more than fifteen minutes without praying." This alleged quote from Wigglesworth implies the idea that a life of prayer rather than moments of prayer was why he saw the power of God released through his ministry.

Additional examples of modern day prayer warriors include Derek Prince, Jack Hayford, James Goll, Dutch Sheets, Cindy Jacobs, Lou Engle, Ana Mendez Ferrell, Dr Peter Wagner, George Otis Jnr. to name a few. You will find me regularly quoting from their books in this prayer guide as their experience and insight is full of wisdom. I also highly recommend you check out the bibliography for book suggestions if you would like to go deeper into the topic of prophetic intercession.

Conclusion

This is a minute portion of the history of prophetic intercession in the church, and yet it reveals a consistent thread of believers seeking to align their prayers with God's heart and purposes, often through what they perceived as divine guidance or revelation. From the early church to modern-day prayer movements, we see a recurring pattern of individuals and communities who have sought to combine deep prayer lives with openness to God's prophetic leading.

As we consider this rich history, may we hold fast to the words of the prophet Jeremiah: "Call to me and I will answer you and tell you great and unsearchable things you do not know" (Jer. 33:3). This invitation to combine prayer with divine revelation can continue to inspire and guide our intercession today.

CHAPTER 3

WEAVING PRAYER INTO LIFE'S FABRIC: CULTIVATING A LIFESTYLE RHYTHM

Introduction

Prophetic intercession is not just a spiritual discipline; it should become a way of life. As we learn to integrate prophetic intercession into our daily routines, we begin to see the world through God's eyes and partner with Him in His purposes, moment by moment. This lifestyle is reflected in 1 Thessalonians 5:17, which exhorts us to "pray without ceasing" (NASB1995).

Biblical Foundations for a Lifestyle of Intercession

1. **Constant prayer**: Luke 18:1 says, "Then Jesus told his disciples a parable to show them that they should always pray and not give up."

2. **Watchfulness**: In Mark 13:33, Jesus instructs, "Be on guard! Be alert! You do not know when that time will come."

3. **Intercession as service**: Samuel states in 1 Samuel 12:23, "As for me, far be it from me that I should sin against the LORD by failing to pray for you."

4. **Spirit-led prayer**: Romans 8:26 reminds us, "In the same way, the Spirit helps us in our weakness. We do not know what we ought to pray for, but the Spirit himself intercedes for us through wordless groans."

Insights from Spiritual Leaders

Beth Moore, author and Bible teacher, shares:

We can be so preoccupied looking to the horizon for the huge thing that we miss the glorious mosaic of a hundred scattered pieces of answered prayer right at our feet. God is rarely up to only one thing.

Our nature is to look for the big finish. His is to call us into constant and daily communion, working through every circumstance, tweaking and turning and tying and telling. He's teaching our tongues the art of tasting in a world trained to binge.

We're looking for the string of pearls. He's planting one pearl here. Another pearl there. The full stretch of our lifetime is the string. We won't see how those jewels all came together on the one strand until we study them under the light of His glorious presence. In the meantime, let's ask God to make us alert and give us eyes to see where He's working on the way to the divine achievement we're longing for.[13]

Key Principles for Cultivating a Lifestyle of Intercession

1. **Develop awareness**: Train yourself to be constantly aware of God's presence and the needs around you.

2. **Practice listening prayer**: Regularly quiet your mind to hear God's voice throughout your day. Often we are simply too busy to recognize His voice, but as we cultivate a culture of

---

[13] Beth Moore, "It's Prayer. That's the Thing," *Living Proof Ministries*, February 4, 2015, https://blog.lproof.org/2015/02/its-prayer-thats-the-thing.html.

listening we can become accustomed to His voice at all times.

3. **Integrate prayer with daily activities**: Turn routine tasks into opportunities for intercession.

4. **Create prayer triggers**: Use daily cues in your environment as reminders to pray.

5. **Cultivate a heart of compassion**: Allow God's love for people to fuel your prayers.

6. **Be flexible**: Be ready to respond to the Holy Spirit's promptings at any moment.

7. **Maintain a prayer journal**: Record insights, answered prayers, and ongoing prayer needs.

Practical Steps to Integrate Prophetic Intercession into Daily Life

1. **Morning consecration**: Start your day by dedicating it to God and asking for prophetic insights.

2. **Prayer walking**: As you walk through your neighborhood or workplace, pray for the people and places you see.

3. **News as prayer prompts**: When you hear news items, immediately lift them up in prayer.

4. **Redeem wait times**: Use times of waiting (in traffic, lines, etc.) as opportunities for intercession.

5. **Pray through your contact list**: Regularly scroll through your phone contacts, praying for each person.

6. **Nighttime review**: End your day by reviewing events and praying over situations you encountered.

7. **Create a prayer space**: Designate a specific area in your home for focused prayer times.

Overcoming Challenges

1. **Busyness**: Remember that prayer can be integrated into activities; it doesn't always require additional time, although it is important to carve out time too!

2. **Distractions**: Practice refocusing your mind on God throughout the day.

3. **Doubt**: Keep a record of answered prayers to boost your faith during dry seasons.

4. **Burnout**: Balance intense intercession with times of rest and receiving from God.

Real-life Example: The Transformation of Almolonga, Guatemala

One powerful example of a lifestyle of intercession comes from the story of Mariano Riscajché, a pastor in Almolonga, Guatemala.[14] In the early 1970s, Almolonga was known as a town plagued by alcoholism, violence, and poverty.

Riscajché felt called by God to pray for his town. He began spending hours each day in prayer, often going to the hills surrounding Almolonga to intercede. He encouraged his congregation to adopt a lifestyle of prayer and fasting for their community.

Over time, other pastors and believers joined in this consistent, passionate intercession for Almolonga. They prayed for specific issues and listened for God's prophetic directions for their prayers.

The results were remarkable. Over the next two decades, Almolonga saw a dramatic transformation:

- Alcoholism rates plummeted, and the town's jails were often empty.
- The economy flourished, particularly in agriculture, with crops yielding abundantly.

---

[14] George Otis, Jr., *Transformations: A Documentary* (New York: The Sentinel Group, 1999), DVD.

- The majority of the population embraced Christianity, and the town became known for its strong family values.

This transformation was documented in several Christian publications and the documentary "Transformation." Riscajché and others attributed these changes directly to the persistent, prophetic intercession that had become a way of life for many in the community.

Practical Exercise: Developing Intercessory Habits

1. Identify 3–5 daily activities you can pair with brief prayers (e.g., brewing coffee, commuting).
2. Set reminders on your phone to pause for a moment of listening prayer throughout the day.
3. Create a prayer map of your local area, assigning specific prayer focuses to different locations.
4. Start a prayer journal, recording daily insights and prayers.
5. Practice turning your worries into prayers immediately when they arise.
6. Share your journey with a prayer partner for mutual encouragement and accountability.

Conclusion

Cultivating a lifestyle of intercession is about aligning our hearts with God's and remaining constantly open to His leading. As you integrate prophetic intercession into your daily life, you'll find that your perspective shifts. Ordinary moments become sacred, and you'll increasingly see the world as God sees it. John Mulinde says it beautifully:

> This ongoing presence of the Lord creates a continuous open heaven surrounding you. It is like walking in a pillar of fire that has come upon your life, and acts as your protection against the spiritual powers of darkness that are at work in the area. It keeps the heavens open above you. If you develop a lifestyle of prayer and allow your heart to become an altar so that no matter where you are or what you are doing, your heart is always praying and conversing with God, you will maintain that fire so that the heavens remain open. Your prayers will not be hindered; they will go straight to the throne of God.[15]

---

[15] John Mulinde and Mark Daniel, *Prayer Altars: A Strategy That Is Changing Nations* (Lake Mary, FL: Creation House, 2013), 122.

As you embrace this lifestyle, may you experience the joy of partnering with God in His purposes, seeing His kingdom come and His will be done on earth as it is in heaven:

And pray in the Spirit on all occasions with all kinds of prayers and requests. With this in mind, be alert and always keep on praying for all the LORD's people. (Eph. 6:18)

CHAPTER 4

HARMONIES FROM HEAVEN: THE SYNERGY OF PROPHETIC INTERCESSION AND WORSHIP

Introduction

Worship, prayer, and intercession are intricately woven together in the tapestry of Scripture.

To worship is the act of honoring and adoring God. In Scripture, it often involves some form of offering, for example through praise in music or gestures of humility such as fasting or sacrifice. Prayer and intercession are communication with God, which can include praise, thanksgiving, confession, and requests.

There is a connection between these elements that is beautifully illustrated in the book of Revelation, particularly through the imagery of harps and bowls. Let's examine some key verses:

And when he had taken it, the four living creatures and the twenty-four elders fell down before the Lamb. Each one had a harp and they were holding golden bowls full of incense, which are the prayers of God's people. (Rev. 5:8)

This verse provides a vivid picture of how worship, prayer, and intercession are intertwined:

- **The harp represents worship**: Throughout Scripture, harps are associated with praise and worship (Ps. 33:2; 150:3). The elders holding harps symbolize continual worship before God's throne.

- **The bowls of incense represent prayer**: Incense rising to heaven is a common biblical metaphor for prayers ascending to God (Ps. 141:2). The bowls full of incense explicitly represent "the prayers of God's people."

- **Intercession is implied**: The elders presenting these prayers before God suggest an intercessory role, bringing the prayers of the saints before the throne.

This interconnection is further reinforced in Revelation 8:3–4:

> Another angel, who had a golden censer, came and stood at the altar. He was given much incense to offer, with the prayers of all God's people, on the golden altar in front of the throne. The smoke of the incense, together with the prayers of God's people, went up before God from the angel's hand.

Here, we see again how the prayers of God's people (including intercession) are mingled with incense and presented as worship before God.

The connection between these elements can be understood as follows:

- Worship can set the atmosphere for effective prayer and intercession. As we honor God through adoration and song, we align our hearts with His will.
- Prayer is itself an act of worship as it acknowledges God's sovereignty and our dependence on Him.
- Intercession often flows out of worship and broader prayer.

- Intercession brings us close to the throne of God and can lead back into more profound attitudes of worship.

This "harp and bowl" model suggests a powerful synergy between worship, prayer, and intercession. It implies that effective prayers and intercessions are saturated with worship, and conversely, that true worship often leads us into deeper prayer and intercession for others.

In practical terms, this could encourage us to incorporate music and praise into prayer times and to view our intercession as an act of worship, allowing our worship to naturally flow into prayer for others.

Biblical Foundations

Old Testament Examples

Moses' intercession on Mount Sinai (Exodus 34:4–9): When the people committed a grave sin of idolatry, the prophet Moses went up the mountain to God to make atonement. He was so overwhelmed by the revelation of the Lord's name that he "bowed to the ground at once and worshiped" (v. 8). And immediately, his adoration led to intercession: "LORD," he said, "if I have found favor in your eyes, then let the LORD go with us. Although this is a stiff-necked people, forgive our wickedness and our sin, and take us as your inheritance" (v. 9).

- **Victory in battle** (2 Chronicles 20:3–22): Faced by an approaching enemy army, King Jehoshaphat summoned all Judah to fast and intercede with him before God. In the midst of their prayer, a prophetic light was granted by the Spirit: "Do not be afraid or discouraged because of this vast army. For the battle is not yours, but God's" (v. 15). The following day, King Jehoshaphat appointed singers to walk ahead of the army, singing to the LORD. As they began to sing and praise, the LORD set ambushes against the enemy, and they were defeated.

- **Worship assembly** (Sirach 50:14–21): Surrounded by the powerful Greek and Roman empires, the nation of Israel fought many battles (both spiritual and military) to defend the heritage of the Lord. Their worship assemblies included both song and sacrifice, adoration and intercession: "All the people together made haste and fell to the ground upon their faces to worship their Lord, the Almighty, God Most High. And the singers praised him with their voices in sweet and full-toned melody. And the people besought the Lord Most High in prayer before him who is merciful, till the order of worship of the Lord was ended" (vv. 17–19).

The Interplay Between Worship and Prophetic Intercession

- **Entering God's presence**: Worship helps us enter God's presence, creating an atmosphere conducive to hearing His voice for intercession.

- **Aligning our hearts**: As we worship, our hearts align with God's, helping us pray according to His will.

- **Spiritual warfare**: Worship can be a powerful weapon in spiritual warfare, often breaking through obstacles in intercession.

- **Prophetic flow**: Worship can stimulate the prophetic flow, leading to inspired prayers and declarations.

- **Sustaining long intercession**: Interspersing worship with intercession can help sustain extended periods of prayer.

The Fiji Revival

In 2004, a remarkable revival broke out in Fiji in the coastal village of Nataleira that many attribute to the combination of worship, repentance, and prophetic intercession.[16] Prior to this revival, groups of intercessors had been gathering regularly to worship and pray for their nation. Crime rates were high; their food source from the ocean was drying up as the reef was dying; and there were demonic strongholds in certain villages. There were even reports of wooden idols that had been placed in villages that would speak demonically and mock people as they walked by!

During an extended few weeks of prayer, repentance, and worship, someone prophesied that God would confirm that He had heard their prayers by bringing a sign of fire. This seemed like an unusual prophecy at the time. However, a few weeks later, fire hit the ocean out of nowhere. The flames were thirty meters high and burned for half an hour. People felt the heat and thought that the water was boiling. However, as the people came closer, they saw that the water was not boiling, but rather it was thousands of fish

---

[16] George Otis, "George Otis and Transformational Revival," interview by Tim Fellows, *Love Black Country*, September 2020, https://www.youtube.com/watch?v=ROgi5o1V7XY.

coming up from the deepest parts of the ocean that they had not seen for decades. The people gathered up as much fish as they could, enough for all eight surrounding villages to be fed. Two fresh water wells also came out of the ground due to the shaking from the fire, and crops were able to be harvested within fifteen days. Many more signs and wonders were recorded as well.

In the following months, Fiji experienced a powerful move of God. Crime rates dropped dramatically, reconciliation occurred between tribal groups, and there were numerous reports of healings and supernatural phenomena. Many Fijians attribute this revival to the persistent, worship-fueled prophetic intercession that preceded it.

Practical Steps to Integrate Worship and Prophetic Intercession

1. **Begin with worship**: Start your intercession times with worship to enter God's presence and align your heart with His.

2. **Use Scripture in song**: Sing scriptures related to your prayer focus, allowing the truth of God's word to fuel your intercession.

3. **Be sensitive to shifts**: Be ready to move between worship and intercession as you feel led by the Holy Spirit.

4. **Create space for spontaneity**: Allow room for spontaneous songs and prayers to emerge during your times of worship and intercession.

5. **Use diverse expressions**: Incorporate various forms or aids in worship (singing, instrumental music, dance, art, incense) to engage different senses and stimulate prophetic flow.

Challenges and Cautions

- **Maintaining focus**: Ensure that the beauty of worship doesn't distract from the purpose of intercession. It is easy to do! Allow your worship to have a specific focus and intentionality.

- **Balancing structure and spontaneity**: Find a healthy balance between planned worship/ prayer and allowing space for spontaneous leading of the Spirit.

- **Avoiding emotional manipulation**: Be cautious not to use music to manipulate emotions rather than genuinely entering God's presence.

Conclusion

The synergy between prophetic intercession and worship creates a powerful dynamic for experiencing God's presence and partnering with His purposes. As we worship, we enter His courts (Ps. 100:4), positioning ourselves to hear His voice and intercede effectively.

As you continue to grow in prophetic intercession, may you discover the deep wells of God's presence that worship unlocks, and may your prayers be enriched by the anthems of heaven.

Part II

THE INTERCESSOR'S TOOLKIT: UNLOCKING DIVINE COMMUNICATION

CHAPTER 5

SPEAKING IN TONGUES: THE LANGUAGE OF THE SPIRIT

Introduction

Speaking in tongues is a spiritual gift mentioned in the New Testament and can be a powerful tool in the arsenal of intercessors. Many report that it leads to strategic spiritual insights and breakthroughs. In my own life I have also found this to be true. This chapter explores the biblical foundations, practical applications, and power of incorporating tongues into prophetic intercession.

Biblical Foundations of Speaking in Tongues

NEW TESTAMENT EXAMPLES

- **Day of Pentecost** (Acts 2:1–4): "When the day of Pentecost came, they were all together in one place. Suddenly a sound like the blowing of a violent wind came from heaven and filled the whole house where they were sitting. They saw what seemed to be tongues of fire that separated and came to rest on each of them. All of them were filled with the Holy Spirit and began to speak in other tongues as the Spirit enabled them."

This event fulfilled what Jesus had promised when He instructed the disciples to wait in Jerusalem until they were "equipped with power from on high" (Luke 24:44–45). In the upper room as the Holy Spirit came upon them, they were filled with this promised power, with the sign of speaking in tongues. Waiting to be filled with the power of the Holy Spirit and then responding to that power in prayer is an important component in becoming a prophetic prayer warrior. How much more will be accomplished through our prayers if we linger with the Lord until we are filled with His gift and our tongues are sanctified—and then pray from that place!

- **Paul's teaching on spiritual gifts** (1 Corinthians 12–14): Summarizing the many spiritual gifts at work in the Christian community, Paul discusses the gift of tongues extensively, particularly in 1 Corinthians 14. Addressing certain abuses that were taking place in the church of Corinth at the time, he explains under what conditions tongues are appropriate in an assembly, i.e., in correlation with the gifts of interpretation and prophecy, "so that the church may be edified" (v. 5). He wanted to encourage them to use these spiritual gifts in a way that was coherent with a life of love and service to others.

- **Mark's Gospel** (Mark 16:17): "And these signs will accompany those who believe: In my name they will drive out demons; they will speak in new tongues."

Understanding Tongues in Prophetic Intercession

Direct Spirit-to-Spirit communication: Speaking in tongues allows for prayer that bypasses the limitations of the mind. Which is not to say that we should not also pray using our understanding, but using both avenues of prayer gives us an advantage:

> For if I pray in a tongue, my spirit prays,
> but my mind is unfruitful. So what shall
> I do? I will pray with my spirit, but I will
> also pray with my understanding; I will sing
> with my spirit, but I will also sing with my
> understanding. (1 Cor. 14:14–15)

Praying the perfect will of God: Tongues is a prayer language, and one of the most powerful aspects of speaking in tongues is being able to pray strategically when we don't know what to pray in English. The Spirit intercedes for us according to God's will:

> In the same way, the Spirit helps us in our
> weakness. We do not know what we ought
> to pray for, but the Spirit himself intercedes
> for us through wordless groans. And he who
> searches our hearts knows the mind of the
> Spirit, because the Spirit intercedes for God's
> people in accordance with the will of God.
> (Rom. 8:26–27)

Spiritual edification: Speaking in tongues edifies the speaker and can potentially be a source of divine insight for the intercessor.

> Anyone who speaks in a tongue edifies themselves. (Cor. 14:4)

Access to divine mysteries: Tongues can provide access to hidden wisdom and revelation, as our spirit communes directly with the Spirit of God:

> For anyone who speaks in a tongue does not speak to people but to God. Indeed, no one understands them; they utter mysteries by the Spirit. (1 Cor. 14:2)

Warfare prayer: Tongues can be a powerful weapon in spiritual warfare, allowing for prayer beyond our understanding.

> And pray in the Spirit on all occasions with all kinds of prayers and requests. With this in mind, be alert and always keep on praying for all the LORD's people. (Eph. 6:18)

Practical Application in Prophetic Intercession

- **Preparation for revelation**: Use tongues to prepare your spirit for receiving prophetic insights.
- **Breakthrough prayer:** When facing spiritual resistance, tongues can break through barriers.
- **Interpretation in intercession**: Seek interpretation of tongues for prophetic direction in prayer.
- **Corporate prayer amplification:** In group settings, tongues can unify and intensify corporate intercession.
- **Personal prayer language:** Develop your prayer language as a daily discipline to enhance your prophetic sensitivity.

Insights from An Experienced Intercessor

Mahesh Chavda shares many valuable insights on the gift of tongues in his book *The Hidden Power of Speaking in Tongues.*

The gift of tongues is a marvelous endowment of the Holy Spirit. It helps us communicate directly with the Lord. Speaking in tongues is the main avenue to our flying higher and swimming deeper in the things of God. It is a special prayer language that connects us with the glory of God, enabling us to pray in the Spirit when we do not know what or how to pray in the weakness and limitation of our human minds. There is no limitation to praying in the Spirit because it taps into the limitless mind of God.[17]

In another portion of his book, he shares on the importance of balance between the spiritual gifts and keeping our eyes on Jesus:

Every spiritual gift and other endowment of the Spirit, including speaking in tongues, is bestowed on believers for the ultimate purpose of equipping and enabling us to bear witness, both individually and corporately, to the saving work of Jesus Christ through His death on the cross and His bodily resurrection. Whenever we begin to focus on spiritual gifts for their own sake, whether tongues or anything else, we are headed for trouble. As Christians we are always in danger of slipping into one or the other of two

---

[17] Mahesh Chavda, *The Hidden Power of Speaking in Tongues* (Shippensburg, PA: Destiny Image Publishers, 2003), 19.

extremes, both equally dangerous. Placing too little emphasis on the gifts and presence of the Holy Spirit robs us of power, while placing too much robs us of vision and direction because it takes our eyes off Jesus.[18]

Modern-Day Example

KENNETH E. HAGIN

Reverend Kenneth Hagin, a teacher, author, and prophet heralding from the faith movement, shares this powerful story after being compelled to intercede:

An intercessor is one who takes the place of another. So when believers stand in the gap and begin to travail in prayer for someone who is lost, sometimes they can feel lost as well...

> On this particular morning, I was kneeling by the sofa and praying when suddenly a strong burden of intercession came over me. At this time, I had only been baptized in the Holy Ghost for 18 months, so the things of the Spirit were new to me. Not knowing what to do with this burden, I just yielded to the Holy Spirit's

---

[18] Chavda, *The Hidden Power of Speaking in Tongues*, 14.

direct unction to groan and to pray in tongues. On the inside of me, in my inner man, I had the sensation of being lost and a sinner. I knew what that felt like because I had been lost only a few years before that! I found myself crying out, "Lost! Lost! Lost! I'm lost! I'm lost!" Of course, I knew I wasn't lost, but I was taking the place of people who were lost. I felt just like they felt, and I was travailing in prayer for them. "I'm lost! Lost!" I cried out as I continued to pray in tongues.

I just know that this time of prayer lasted for quite some time. Then that evening in the church service, I had only been preaching for 15 minutes when right in the middle of my sermon, the power of God fell. Every single sinner in the house got saved, and every backslider recommitted his life that night. Not a single one of them was left out! That's what I had been praying about earlier that day. I had been interceding for those unsaved people.[19]

---

[19] Kenneth Hagin, *Tongues—Beyond the Upper Room*, (Broken Arrow, OK: RHEMA Bible Church, 2007), 228–29.

Scientific Evidence

Speaking in tongues now has science backing up what believers have known all along. Recent brain imaging studies have shed light on what is happening when people engage in this spiritual practice.

The research conducted by Dr. Andrew Newberg's reveals some fascinating changes in the brain during *glossolalia* (speaking in tongues). When people start speaking in tongues, the part of their brain responsible for self-control takes a backseat. At the same time, the area that helps us connect with our surroundings and process sensory information kicks into high gear.

What does this mean? Essentially, the brain enters a unique state where people feel like they are letting go of control and experiencing a deeper connection with the Lord. It's different from meditation, where focus of the mind is required. With tongues, it's more about releasing and receiving.

This research provides some solid evidence for why speaking in tongues can be such an effective tool for prayer and prophetic intercession. It creates a mental state that's primed for spiritual experience and could explain why many receive direct messages from God during their prayer times. This is perfect when we want to pray what God wants to pray—on earth as it is in Heaven, rather than our own ideas. For this reason, speaking in tongues can be a very valuable tool in our prayer life.[20]

Practical Exercises and Activations

- **Tongues journal:** Keep a journal nearby when praying in tongues. Write down any impressions, visions, or interpretations that come during or after these prayer times.
- **Group tongues activation:** In a group setting, designate periods for corporate prayer in tongues, followed by a time of sharing prophetic impressions received.
- **Tongues and Scripture meditation:** Combine praying in tongues with meditation on specific scriptures, allowing the Spirit to illuminate the Word prophetically.

Conclusion

Speaking in tongues in prophetic intercession is a powerful convergence of two spiritual gifts. It allows intercessors to pray beyond their natural

---

[20] Constance Holden, "Tongues on the Mind," *Science,* November 2, 2006, https://www.science.org/content/article/tongues-mind.

understanding, which can lead to profound prophetic insights and breakthroughs. As we learn to integrate tongues into our prophetic prayer lives, we open ourselves to deeper realms of spiritual discernment and effectiveness in intercession. Remember, the goal is not just supernatural experiences, but partnering with God's heart and purposes for individuals, communities, and nations.

CHAPTER 6

VISIONS AND DREAMS: RECEIVING DIVINE INTEL

Introduction

*I*n the realm of prophetic intercession, dreams and visions serve as powerful tools that God uses to communicate His heart and strategies to His people. Throughout Scripture and history, we see how God has used these divine encounters to guide, warn, and inspire His intercessors. This chapter explores the significance of dreams and visions in prayer and intercession, providing biblical foundations, modern-day examples, and practical exercises to help you discern and apply these revelations in your prayer life.

Biblical Foundations of Dreams and Visions in Intercession

OLD TESTAMENT EXAMPLES

- **Abraham's visions**: (Genesis 12–22): God appears to Abraham in many visions, reaffirming His covenant and promising descendants who will inherit the land, which can be seen as an intercessory vision for future generations.

- **Joseph the dreamer** (Genesis 37–47): Joseph's prophetic dreams and his ability to interpret them not only shaped his personal destiny but also saved nations from famine.

- **Daniel's visions** (Daniel 7–12): Daniel received numerous visions that provided insight into future events and prompted him to intercede for his people.

NEW TESTAMENT EXAMPLES

- **Peter's vision** (Acts 10:9–16): Peter's vision of unclean animals challenged his prejudices (Acts 10:17–48), and those of his fellow Jewish Christians (Acts 11:1–18) and opened the door for the Gospel to reach the Gentiles.

- **Paul's vision of the Macedonian man** (Acts 16:9–10): This vision redirected Paul's missionary journey, impacting the spread of Christianity in Europe.
- **John's revelations** (Revelation 1–22): The entire book of Revelation is a series of visions given to John, providing insight into spiritual realities and future events.

The Purpose of Dreams and Visions in Intercession

- **Revelation of God's will:** Dreams and visions can reveal God's specific plans, allowing intercessors to align their prayers with His purposes.
- **Warning and preparation**: God may use dreams to warn of coming dangers or challenges, prompting intercessors to stand in the gap.
- **Encouragement and confirmation:** Visions can provide encouragement to persevere in prayer or confirm that intercessors are on the right track.
- **Strategic insight:** Dreams may reveal specific strategies or approaches to take in prayer and spiritual warfare.

- **Global perspective:** Visions can provide insight into situations in other parts of the world, expanding the intercessor's prayer focus.

Modern-Day Examples

REES HOWELLS' VISION OF THE WAR

On December 26, 1934, Welsh intercessor Rees Howells received a vision concerning world evangelism and fulfilling the great commission.[21] This led him and his team into sessions of intense intercession prior to and throughout World War II. Historian Klaus Fischer in his book Nazi Germany: A New History writes:

> Remembering the miracle of Dunkirk, acknowledged by various leaders to be an intervention from God—the calm sea allowing the smallest boats to cross, the almost complete evacuation of English troops—and then the lead Mr. Churchill gave to the nation, how thankful we are that God had this company of hidden intercessors whose lives were on the

---

[21] Matt Lockett, "Rees Howells: How Prayers Played a Role in Ending Hitler's Reign of Death," *Justice House of Prayer DC*, accessed September 20, 2024, https://www.jhopdc.com/rees-howells-part-2.

altar day after day as they stood in the gap for the deliverance of Britain.[22]

Grubb in his biography on Howells comments:

> After the war, Air Chief Marshal Lord Dowding, Commander-in-Chief of Fighter Command in the Battle of Britain, made this significant comment: "Even during the battle one realized from day to day how much external support was coming in. At the end of the battle one had the sort of feeling that there had been some special Divine intervention to alter some sequence of events which would otherwise have occurred."[23]

RICK JOYNER'S THE FINAL QUEST

Rick Joyner has written extensively about his visions and their impact on his ministry and intercession in his book *The Final Quest*. Joyner describes a series of visions that provided insight into spiritual warfare and the state of the church. This book deeply impacted me in my early years of ministry. Joyner's visions led him to establish intercession teams and prophetic training programs, influencing many in the charismatic and prophetic movements

---

[22] Klaus Fischer, *Nazi Germany: A New History* (New York: Continuum, 1995), 456–57.

[23] Grubb, *Rees Howells: Intercessor,* 262.

to integrate dreams and visions into their prayer lives.

Discerning and Interpreting Dreams and Visions

- **Align with Scripture:** Always test dreams and visions against the Word of God. Genuine revelations will never contradict Scripture.

- **Seek wisdom:** Proverbs 11:14 reminds us, "Where there is no guidance, a people falls, but in an abundance of counselors there is safety" (ESV). Share your dreams and visions with mature believers for insight and confirmation.

- **Look for patterns:** God often speaks through recurring themes or symbols in dreams. Keep a journal to track these patterns.

- **Pray for interpretation:** Just as Daniel prayed for understanding of his visions, ask God for clarity and insight into what He's showing you.

- **Consider the context:** Dreams and visions often relate to current circumstances or concerns in your life or the world around you.

Practical Exercises and Activations

- **Dream journal:** Keep a notebook by your bed to record dreams immediately upon waking. Write down as many details as you can remember, including emotions, colors, and symbols.

- **Vision board for intercession:** Create a visual representation of the dreams and visions God has given you for your areas of intercession. Use images, scriptures, and words that capture these revelations.

- **Guided imagery prayer:** Spend time in quiet prayer, asking God to show you images or scenes related to your area of intercession. Allow your imagination to be guided by the Holy Spirit, then pray into what you see.

- **Group dream interpretation:** In a small group, share recent dreams and practice interpreting them together, using biblical principles and seeking the Holy Spirit's guidance.

- **Prophetic act based on a vision:** If you've received a vision related to your area of intercession, create a symbolic act to physically express what you've seen. This could involve using props, creating art, or performing a specific action as you pray.

Conclusion

Dreams and visions are not just mystical experiences; they are practical tools that God uses to equip and guide His intercessors. As we cultivate sensitivity to His voice and learn to steward these revelations, we become more effective partners with God in seeing His will done on earth as it is in heaven. Remember, the goal is not just to have exciting spiritual experiences, but to use these divine insights to fuel passionate, targeted intercession that aligns with God's heart and purposes.

CHAPTER 7

PRAYER BEYOND WORDS: CREATIVE EXPRESSIONS OF PRAYER

Introduction

*P*rophetic intercession doesn't always have to follow traditional prayer formats. God, the ultimate Creator, can inspire us to use creative means to express our prayers and prophetic insights. As we explore various artistic and experiential methods of intercession, we open ourselves to new dimensions of connecting with God and interceding for others.

Biblical Foundations for Creative Ways to Worship (and Intercede)

Music and worship: 2 Kings 3:15–16 describes how the prophet Elisha called for a musician before prophesying:

> "But now bring me a harpist." While the harpist was playing, the hand of the LORD came on Elisha and he said, "This is what the LORD says..."

Visual arts: In Ezekiel 4:1–3, God instructs Ezekiel to create a visual representation of Jerusalem under siege as a prophetic act:

> "Now, son of man, take a block of clay, put it in front of you and draw the city of Jerusalem on it . . ."

Dance: 2 Samuel 6:14 shows David using dance as a form of worship and prophetic declaration:

> Wearing a linen ephod, David was dancing before the LORD with all his might.

Drama and symbolic acts: Jeremiah was often instructed to perform symbolic acts as part of his prophetic ministry. For instance, in Jeremiah 19:10–

11, he was told to buy a clay jar and smash it in front of the elders and priests as a prophetic sign:

> "Then break the jar while those who go with you are watching, and say to them, 'This is what the LORD Almighty says: I will smash this nation and this city just as this potter's jar is smashed and cannot be repaired. They will bury the dead in Topheth until there is no more room.'"

Creative Methods of Prophetic Intercession

MUSIC AND WORSHIP

Music can be a powerful tool for entering God's presence and expressing prophetic prayers. This can include:

- Spontaneous worship songs
- Instrumental intercession
- Prophetic songwriting

Julie Meyer, Dove-nominated artist and worship leader at the International House of Prayer, often engages in what she calls "singing the scriptures." In her book, *Singing the Scriptures: How All Believers Can Experience Breakthrough, Hope and Healing,* she takes Scripture passages and spontaneously creates melodies and songs as a form of prophetic intercession. What a powerful way to pray![24]

VISUAL ARTS

Creating visual art can be a profound way to express prophetic insights and prayers. This might involve:

- Painting or drawing during prayer times
- Creating prophetic banners or flags
- Sculpting or working with clay

In her book *The Creative Call: An Artist's Response to the Way of the Spirit,* Janice Elsheimer describes a woman who felt led to create a painting during a time of intercessory prayer for her church.[25] The resulting artwork depicted a tree with deep roots and abundant fruit, which later became a powerful prophetic message of encouragement for the congregation.

MOVEMENT AND DANCE

Physical movement can express prayers that words cannot. Several psalms mention dance as a form of worship. For example:

---

[24] Julie Meyer, *Singing the Scriptures: How All Believers Can Experience Breakthrough, Hope and Healing* (Minneapolis: Chosen Books, 2018).

[25] Janice Elsheimer, *The Creative Call: An Artist's Response to the Way of the Spirit* (Colorado Springs: WaterBrook Press, 2001).

> Let them praise his name with dancing and
> make music to him with timbrel and harp.
> (Ps. 149:3)

> Praise him with timbrel and dancing, praise
> him with the strings and pipe. (Ps. 150:4)

In Exodus 15:20–21, Miriam led the women in dance and song after the Israelites crossed the Red Sea, celebrating God's deliverance. David danced "with all his might" before the Ark of the Covenant as it was brought into Jerusalem (2 Sam. 6:14–15). During the Feast of Tabernacles, the Israelites were instructed to "take branches from luxuriant trees . . . and rejoice before the LORD your God for seven days" (Lev. 23:40), waving these branches in celebration. Likewise, the march around Jericho in Joshua 6:1–20 is a powerful example of symbolic movement in warfare prayer. These are examples of prayer in movement.

The idea of prayer in movement and dance could include:

- Interpretive dance
- Flag or banner waving
- Symbolic walking or marching prayers

WRITING AND JOURNALING

Creative writing can be a form of prophetic intercession. This might involve:

- Poetry
- Prophetic journaling
- Writing letters to God or from God's perspective

Madeline L'Engle, author of one of my favorite books, *Walking on Water: Reflections on Faith and Art*, compares her approach to writing as the same as her approach to prayer:

> To work on a book is for me very much the same thing as to pray. Both involve discipline. If the artist works only when he feels like it, he's not apt to build up much of a body of work. Inspiration far more often comes during the work than before it, because the largest part of the job of the artist is to listen to the work and to go where it tells him to go. Ultimately, when you are writing, you stop thinking and write what you hear.

> To pray is to listen also, to move through my own chattering to God to that place where I can be silent and listen to what God may have to say. But if I pray only when I feel like it, God may choose not to speak. The greatest moments

of prayer come in the midst of fumbling and faltering prayer rather than at the odd moment when one decides to try to turn to God.[26]

DRAMA AND PROPHETIC ACTS

Engaging in dramatic representations or symbolic acts can be powerful forms of intercession. This could include:

- The acting out of biblical scenes (theater presentations, etc.)
- Performing prophetic gestures
- Creating and walking through prayer stations

These dramatic and symbolic approaches to prayer draw inspiration from biblical examples and have been adopted by many contemporary Christian traditions. They offer a visceral, multisensory way to engage with spiritual concepts and communicate with God. Such acts can serve multiple purposes: they can be forms of personal or communal prayer, tools for teaching and reflection, and means of prophetic proclamation.

---

[26] Madeleine L'Engle, *Walking on Water: Reflections on Faith and Art* (New York: Convergent Books, 2016), 140.

A LESSON FROM EZEKIEL

In Ezekiel 4:1–8 God instructs Ezekiel to perform a dramatic act as a form of prophetic prayer and proclamation:

- Ezekiel was told to take a clay tablet and draw a picture of Jerusalem on it.
- He was then instructed to "lay siege" to this representation of the city by building siege works against it, erecting a ramp, setting up camps, and placing battering rams around it.
- Ezekiel was then told to take an iron pan and place it as an iron wall between himself and the city.
- He was instructed to face the city and bear the sin of Israel by lying on his left side for 390 days, and then on his right side for 40 days, each day representing a year of punishment for Israel and Judah respectively.
- During this time, he was to prophesy against Jerusalem.

This act was both a form of intercessory prayer and a dramatic prophecy about the coming siege and fall of Jerusalem. It served as a visual representation of God's message to the people, making the abstract concept of judgment more concrete and visceral.

From Ezekiel's symbolic siege in the Old Testament to modern prayer walks and interactive prayer stations, these practices demonstrate the diverse and creative ways believers have sought to deepen their prayer lives and express their faith. By engaging the body and imagination alongside the intellect and spirit, drama and prophetic acts in prayer can create powerful, memorable experiences that resonate with participants and observers alike.

Culinary Intercession

As strange as it may sound, I would like to propose that even our food preparation and eating can become acts of prophetic intercession. All we do can be a spiritual service to the Lord. This might involve:

- Fasting from or eating specific foods as prayer acts
- Preparing meals prayerfully for others
- Communion as a form of intercession

In Acts 10, Peter's vision of a sheet filled with all kinds of animals was a profound prophetic message about the inclusion of Gentiles in God's plan.

Culinary intercession recognizes the spiritual significance of food and eating in the Christian tradition. It draws on the rich symbolism of meals in Scripture and incorporates food-related practices into prayer and spiritual warfare. This approach to intercession engages multiple senses and can create powerful, memorable experiences that deepen one's connection with God and others.

ADDITIONAL EXAMPLES AND PRACTICES:

1. **Prayer before meals:** The traditional practice of praying before meals and asking God to bless the food we receive allows for every meal to be used as an occasion to share with intention in thankfulness for God's providence.

2. **Prophetic eating**: Consuming specific foods to symbolize spiritual truths or declarations. For instance, eating honey to declare God's sweetness over a situation, or bitter herbs to acknowledge hardship while praying for deliverance.

3. **Prayer feasts**: Organizing meals where each dish represents a specific prayer focus or attribute of God, allowing participants to "consume" these prayers physically and spiritually.

4. **Fasting as intercession**: Abstaining from food (or specific foods) for a set period while focusing prayer on particular needs or issues.

5. **Breaking bread for unity**: Sharing meals across cultural or denominational lines as a form of intercessory action for church unity.

6. **Anointed cooking**: Praying over ingredients and the cooking process, infusing meals with intentional blessings and intercessions for those who will consume them.

THEOLOGICAL FOUNDATIONS:

- **The Last Supper and Communion** (Matthew 26:26–28): Jesus used bread and wine as powerful symbols of His body and blood, establishing a lasting connection between food and spiritual realities.

- **Fasting in the Bible** (e.g., Esther 4:16; Matthew 6:16–18): Scripture often connects fasting with intense prayer and seeking God's intervention.

- **Hospitality as a spiritual gift** (Romans 12:13; 1 Peter 4:9): The preparation and sharing of food is seen as a way to serve others and honor God.

- **Diversity of devotions** (Romans 14:1–6): Paul teaches that believers should respect diverse practices and convictions about dietary choices and sacred days, recognizing that both those who eat freely and those who abstain can do so as an act of devotion to God, without judging one another.

CONTEMPORARY APPLICATIONS:

- Prayer ministries organizing "prayer banquets" where each course represents a different aspect of intercession.
- Intentional use of cultural foods in cross-cultural ministry as a form of bridging prayer.
- Integration of mindful eating practices with contemplative prayer traditions.

CAUTIONS AND CONSIDERATIONS:

- Avoid superstitious thinking or attributing magical properties to food.
- Be sensitive to those with eating disorders or food-related health issues.
- Maintain the focus on God and prayer, rather than on the food itself.

This might be an unusual way to pray, but it also can serve as a multisensory reminder that God is in all things, and by being creative with the way we pray, we allow God to encompass all our senses, which can include eating and drinking. By integrating culinary elements into intercession, believers can engage in holistic prayer experiences that nourish both body and spirit, creating tangible expressions of faith and facilitating deeper connections with God and community.

Implementing Creative Prophetic Intercession

1. **Stay Scripture-centered**: Ensure all creative expressions align with biblical truth.
2. **Remain humble**: Remember that the goal is effective prayer, not artistic showcase.
3. **Be open to the Spirit**: Allow the Holy Spirit to guide your creative expressions.
4. **Interpret and apply**: Seek to understand and apply any insights gained through creative intercession.
5. **Community discernment**: Share your creative prophetic insights with mature believers for confirmation and interpretation.

Overcoming Challenges

1. **Self-consciousness**: Remember that your audience is God, not other people.
2. **Lack of artistic skill**: Creative intercession is about the heart, not artistic perfection.
3. **Unusual methods**: Be prepared to explain the biblical basis for creative intercession to those who might not understand.

Conclusion

Creative expressions in prophetic intercession open up new avenues for connecting with God's heart and expressing His purposes. God is the source of all creativity, and He delights in using our creative expressions as vehicles for His prophetic purposes. As you engage in creative prophetic intercession, may you discover new depths in your prayer life and new avenues for expressing God's heart for the world.

CHAPTER 8

DIVINE METAPHOR: HARNESSING THE POWER OF PROPHETIC ACTS AND SYMBOLS

Introduction

Prophetic acts and symbols are powerful tools in intercessory prayer, often serving as physical representations of realities in the spirit. These acts can be deeply meaningful, helping to engage our whole being in prayer and serving as a point of faith for breakthrough. As we explore this dimension of prophetic intercession, let's reflect on Jeremiah 1:11–12:

> The word of the LORD came to me: "What do you see, Jeremiah?" "I see the branch of an almond tree," I replied. The LORD said to me,

"You have seen correctly, for I am watching to see that my word is fulfilled."

Just as God used a simple almond branch to convey a profound message to Jeremiah, our prophetic acts in prayer can become conduits for divine revelation and catalysts for the fulfillment of God's promises.

Using physical items as a prophetic act has biblical precedent. In the book of Acts, we see a powerful example of this practice:

God did extraordinary miracles through Paul, so that even handkerchiefs and aprons that had touched him were taken to the sick, and their illnesses were cured and the evil spirits left them. (Acts 19:11–12)

This account demonstrates how ordinary objects became a "touch point" for God's healing power and can be used in connection with prayer as a prophetic act.

In modern practice, believers might use:

- **Prayer shawls:** Knitted or crocheted with prayer, sent to those needing comfort or healing.

- **Anointed objects:** Items prayed over for specific purposes (e.g., a toy for a sick child, a key for a new home).
- **Communion elements:** Bread and wine/juice as powerful symbols of Christ's sacrifice.
- **Written prayers or Scripture:** Placed in significant locations or carried by individuals.

These practices remind us that God can use tangible, physical means to manifest His spiritual power. However, it's crucial to maintain focus on God as the source of power, rather than attributing special properties to the objects themselves. The items serve as points of contact, helping build faith and create a physical connection to prayer and intercession.

Biblical Foundations

OLD TESTAMENT EXAMPLES

- **Moses' staff**: In Exodus 14:16, God instructs Moses, "Raise your staff and stretch out your hand over the sea to divide the water so that the Israelites can go through the sea on dry ground."
- **Joshua and Jericho**: Joshua 6:3–5 describes the prophetic act of marching around Jericho: "March around the city once with all the armed

men. Do this for six days. Have seven priests carry trumpets of rams' horns in front of the ark. On the seventh day, march around the city seven times, with the priests blowing the trumpets. When you hear them sound a long blast on the trumpets, have the whole army give a loud shout; then the wall of the city will collapse and the army will go up, everyone straight in."

- **Elisha's arrows**: In 2 Kings 13:15–19, Elisha instructs the king to shoot arrows and then strike the ground with them as a prophetic act symbolizing victory over Aram.

- **Isaiah's nakedness**: Isaiah 20:2–4 recounts God instructing Isaiah to walk naked and barefoot for three years as a prophetic sign against Egypt and Cush.

- **Jeremiah's yoke**: In Jeremiah 27:2, God tells Jeremiah to make a yoke and wear it as a prophetic symbol of Babylon's rule.

NEW TESTAMENT EXAMPLES

- **Jesus using mud:** In John 9:6–7, Jesus heals a blind man by anointing his eyes with mud from dirt and saliva.

- **Anointing oil:** Mark 6:13 and James 5:14 tell us that oils were used in healing the sick.
- **Anointing of Jesus at Bethany:** All four Gospels recount the anointing of Jesus with precious aromatic nard (Matt. 26:7–13; Mark 14:3–9; Luke 7:37–50; John 12:3–8), to which he attributes the prophetic value of preparing him for burial.

Types of Prophetic Acts and Symbols

1. **Physical objects**: Using items like swords, flags, or stones in prayer.
2. **Bodily actions**: Kneeling, dancing, or laying prostrate during intercession.
3. **Spoken declarations**: Making verbal proclamations or decrees.
4. **Written words**: Writing down prayers or scriptures as an act of faith.
5. **Artistic expressions**: Creating or using art, music, or dance in intercession.
6. **Symbolic journeys**: Prayer walks or pilgrimages to specific locations.

The Purpose of Prophetic Acts and Symbols

1. **Faith activation**: Physical acts can help activate and express faith.
2. **Spiritual warfare**: Symbols can be powerful in spiritual battles—much like an emblem on a shield, etc.
3. **Revelation:** Acts can lead to deeper understanding of God's purposes.
4. **Breakthrough:** Prophetic acts can be catalysts for spiritual breakthroughs.
5. **Remembrance:** Symbols serve as memorials of God's promises and actions.

Modern-Day Examples

THE FFALD-Y-BRENIN RETREAT CENTER STORY:

The book *The Grace Outpouring: Becoming a People of Blessing* details the story of a Christian retreat center in Wales where the miraculous takes place. The book is filled with incredible stories of God bringing healing to the many hundreds of people who visit the retreat center every year. The practice of "blessing the land" through prayer walks and declarations led to numerous reported healings and spiritual transformations in the local community. The authors describe how they would walk the boundaries of the property, pouring out small amounts of oil and praying blessings over the land and people. They report that this practice coincided with an increase in unexpected visitors experiencing spiritual encounters and physical healings.[27]

I love this report:

> One profoundly deaf visitor was concerned shortly before leaving that he had lost his essential hearing-aid. To his great surprise it suddenly dawned on him that during his stay his hearing had returned completely and his hearing-aid was now redundant! Recently a young blind mother, with several children at home whom she had never seen, received her sight. What a joyful homecoming there must have been in that household![28]

Here are some other examples of how prophetic acts and symbols can have powerful repercussions. These are not true stories, but ideas that may inspire you:

[27] Roy Godwin and Dave Roberts, *The Grace Outpouring: Becoming a People of Blessing* (Colorado Springs: David C. Cook, 2012).

[28] Richard Sutton, "Ffald-y-Brenin – A Place of Blessing," *A Listening Heart*, accessed September 12, 2024, https://alisteningheart.blog/2018/08/01/ffald-y-brenin-a-place-of-blessing/.

THE PRAYER SHAWL MINISTRY

Imagine Sarah, a retired nurse. She felt called to start a prayer shawl ministry in her church. She and a group of volunteers would knit or crochet shawls while praying for the recipients. One day, they created a shawl for Mark, a young man battling cancer. As they worked, they prayed for healing and comfort. When Mark received the shawl, he was deeply moved. He later shared that whenever he wore it during chemotherapy sessions, he felt a tangible sense of peace and God's presence. Remarkably, his treatment was more successful than doctors initially expected, and he attributed this in part to the prayers infused in the shawl.

THE ANOINTED KEY

Imagine Rachel, a real estate agent and intercessor, who had been trying to sell a property that had been on the market for over a year. Feeling led by the Holy Spirit, she took a key similar to the one for the house and anointed it with oil, praying over it for a week. She declared that God would bring the right buyer who would use the property for His purposes.

Within days of this act, a Christian non-profit organization contacted her, looking for a space to start a community center. They ended up purchasing the property, and it has since become a thriving hub for ministry and outreach in the neighborhood.

THE PROPHETIC ART INSTALLATION

David, an artist and intercessor, felt burdened for his city's homeless population. He created an art installation featuring a large, empty picture frame in the city center. He invited passersby to write prayers for the homeless on small pieces of paper and attach them to the frame. Over a month, the frame filled with hundreds of prayers. This visual representation of intercession caught the attention of local media and city officials. As a result, new initiatives were launched to address homelessness, and many churches became more actively involved in serving this population.

THE HEALING STONES

During a conference on healing and intercession, attendees were given small stones and encouraged to write the names of people needing healing on them. These stones were collected and placed in a basket at the altar. The intercessors prayed over the basket throughout the weekend. Months later, testimonies began pouring in from people whose names were on those stones, reporting miraculous healings and answers to prayer. The conference organizers now keep the basket of stones in their prayer room as a continual reminder of God's faithfulness and the power of intercessory prayer.

Guidelines for Prophetic Acts and Symbols

1. **Seek God's guidance**: Ensure the act is led by the Holy Spirit, not personal imagination.
2. **Scriptural alignment**: The act should align with biblical principles.
3. **Humility**: Perform acts with a humble heart, not for show or personal glory.
4. **Wisdom**: Consider the cultural context and potential impact of public acts.
5. **Faith**: Believe in the spiritual significance of the act, even if results aren't immediately visible.

Practical Exercise: Engaging in Prophetic Acts

1. Pray for guidance on a specific issue requiring intercession.
2. Ask God if there's a symbolic act He wants you to perform related to this issue.

3. If led to do so, carry out the act with faith and reverence.
4. Journal about the experience, including any insights or scriptures that come to mind.
5. Continue to pray and watch for results related to your act of intercession.

Conclusion

Prophetic acts and symbols in intercession are not magical rituals, but faith-filled actions that engage our whole being in prayer. They can serve as powerful points of contact between the natural and spiritual realms. May your prophetic acts be led by the Holy Spirit, grounded in Scripture, and filled with faith, as you partner with God in seeing His kingdom come on earth as it is in heaven.

CHAPTER 9
PRAYING ON LOCATION: LANDMARKS AS LAUNCHPADS

Introduction

Praying from landmarks is a powerful yet often overlooked aspect of prophetic intercession. This practice involves using physical locations as focal points for prayer, drawing on their historical, spiritual, or symbolic significance. As we explore this concept, we'll see how God has used landmarks throughout biblical history and how we can incorporate this practice into our modern-day intercession.

Biblical Foundations

OLD TESTAMENT EXAMPLES

- **Daniel's window prayer**: In Daniel 6:10, we see Daniel praying toward Jerusalem from his window: "Now when Daniel learned that the decree had been published, he went home to his upstairs room where the windows opened toward Jerusalem. Three times a day he got down on his knees and prayed, giving thanks to his God, just as he had done before."

- **Solomon's Temple dedication**: In 1 Kings 8:29–30, Solomon prays, "May your eyes be open toward this temple night and day, this place of which you said, 'My Name shall be there,' so that you will hear the prayer your servant prays toward this place. Hear the supplication of your servant and of your people Israel when they pray toward this place."

- **Abraham's altars**: Throughout Genesis, we see Abraham building altars at significant locations. For example, Genesis 12:7 states, "The LORD appeared to Abram and said, 'To your offspring I will give this land.' So he built an altar there to the LORD, who had appeared to him."

NEW TESTAMENT EXAMPLES

- **John's ministry at the Jordan:** Mark 1:5 tells us that all of Judea gathered to be baptized by John at the Jordan river. This location lent prophetic meaning to the gesture, as it marked Israel's crossing-over from slavery and sin into the Lord's promised inheritance.

- **Annual pilgrimages to Jerusalem:** The Gospels tell us that Jesus went annually to Jerusalem for the major feasts, both as a child with his parents and later as a master with his disciples. When the hour of his death grew near, he said, "I must go on my way today and tomorrow and the day following, for it cannot be that a prophet should perish away from Jerusalem" (Luke 13:33, ESV).

- **Jesus at the Mount of Olives:** Luke 22:39–41 shows Jesus' habit of praying at a specific location: "Jesus went out as usual to the Mount of Olives, and his disciples followed him. On reaching the place, he said to them, 'Pray that you will not fall into temptation.' He withdrew about a stone's throw beyond them, knelt down and prayed."

Key Principles in Praying from Landmarks

1. **Recognizing spiritual significance:** Understand that certain places can hold spiritual significance due to historical events, divine encounters, or prophetic declarations.
2. **Aligning with God's purposes:** Use landmarks as reminders of God's past works and promises for the future.
3. **Engaging the spiritual realm:** Physical locations can serve as points of contact between the natural and spiritual realms.
4. **Declaring God's will:** Use landmarks as platforms for making prophetic declarations over regions or nations.
5. **Remembrance and gratitude:** Landmarks can serve as memorials, helping us remember God's faithfulness and stirring gratitude.

Practical Steps in Praying from Landmarks

1. **Research:** Study the history and significance of landmarks in your area or places you're led to pray for.

2. **Discern:** Ask the Holy Spirit for guidance on which landmarks to focus on and how to pray.
3. **Visit:** When possible, physically visit the landmark to pray on-site.
4. **Visualize:** If unable to visit, use maps or images to visualize the location during prayer.
5. **Declare:** Make faith-filled declarations based on the landmark's significance and your prophetic insights.
6. **Journal:** Record your experiences, insights, and any perceived spiritual shifts after praying from landmarks.

Real-life Examples

THE WESTERN WALL, JERUSALEM

The Western Wall in Jerusalem, also known as the Wailing Wall, has been a significant prayer landmark for centuries. Jews from around the world come to pray at this remnant of the ancient temple, believing it to be the closest accessible site to the Holy of Holies. Many Christians also visit to pray, recognizing its historical and spiritual significance.

PRAYER IN THE SWEDISH REGION OF BERGSLAGEN

Dr. Peter Wagner, in his book *Breaking Spiritual Strongholds in Your City*, shares the powerful story of the Swedish region of Bergslagen, where a remarkable demonstration of the power of strategic prayer unfolded, transforming a community gripped by economic despair and spiritual darkness into one renewed with hope and prosperity.

There was a decline in church and many were unemployed. The iron mill that employed 600 workers was shut down. A protest led to the entire town turning off all electricity in their homes, streets, and stores. The news report on television dramatically showed the town in complete darkness. Property prices fell, and selling a house was almost impossible. During this time Dr. Wagner and his team spent six months of prayer in total dedication to this region.

> My friend Lars Widerberg, the spy in our prayer team, did the spiritual mapping and discovered there were 15 New Age centers in the area.[29] Every time through history when our nation's freedom had been threatened, the farmers from Bergslagen became the freedom fighters who saved the country. Bergslagen was

---

[29] "Spiritual Mapping" is a phrase coined by George Otis, Jr. Part of the process of spiritual mapping involves asking the Lord for any prophetic words or visions concerning what is happening in a region and studying the history of a region to find any points or links that can be prayed for. It involves research to see where Satan may have a foothold in preventing the Lord moving.

the birthplace of industry in Sweden and now it was heading for oblivion.

The first factory in Sweden's history was now occupied by a community connected with the Findhorn Foundation from England, which confesses that Lucifer is their source of power. We went into the Lucifer center and had coffee. To outsiders we appeared as a group in pleasant conversation while we were looking into the eyes of one another and proclaiming the Lordship of Jesus over the community. Two months later four members of that community came to the Lord and were filled with the Holy Spirit. The Lord gave us the spoils from our prayer action.

Lars also discovered that in the Bergslagen area lived a spiritist medium who claimed to be a channel for the spirit of Jambres, an Egyptian who had lived 3,000 years ago. We organized a prayer bus filled with intercessors and stopped outside of every New Age center in the city to pray. The prayer bus also stopped outside every town hall in the area. We prayed that the local political leadership would receive wisdom from God to solve the problems of unemployment in the area. We prayed that they would use public funds with wisdom and honesty. We did spiritual warfare against the spirit of Jambres. Jambres was one of the Egyptian magicians who withstood Moses and Aaron to hinder the Exodus from Egypt.

We had a tough battle and went through a fire of opposition from the local media, who could not understand our boldness to proclaim a new day for Bergslagen. That evening when we directly challenged the spirit of Jambres, opposition started and increased until the weekend when we proclaimed a new day for Bergslagen. The opposition helped us believe that we had hit the target. Jambres may well have been the territorial spirit over the area.

The day after the victory proclamation the government gave a grant of one billion Swedish crowns (150 million U.S. dollars) to the whole area. Immediately prices of property went up and unemployment went down. The iron mill closed, but all the workers got new jobs. Our prayer action drew pastors and churches into unity and they kept on praying together. When the media reported the changes in the area, they used the same words we had used in our prayer proclamations, but of course they reported no cause-and-effect relationships.[30]

ALBANIA AND DENMARK

Dr. Wagner shares another powerful story about intercession on the borders of Albania and Denmark:

I led prayer teams that prayed at the borders of Albania. Others did similar prayer actions. Before Denmark had its referendum, when the majority voted no to the Maastrich agreement to a European union, intercessors did prayer walks along the border between Germany and Denmark because they sensed that the agreement would be a setback for the gospel.[31]

THE REVIVAL POOLS OF WALES

During the Welsh Revival of 1904–1905, certain locations became known as "revival pools"—places where the presence of God seemed particularly strong. Intercessors would gather at these landmarks to pray for the continuation and spread of revival. The Moriah Chapel in Loughor, where Evan Roberts first experienced a powerful move of God, became one such landmark.[32]

---

[30] C. Peter Wagner, *Breaking Spiritual Strongholds in Your City* (Shippensburg, PA: Destiny Image Publishers, 1993), 97–99.

[31] Wagner, *Breaking Spiritual Strongholds in Your City,* 100.

[32] W. T. Stead, "Evan Roberts," in *The Welsh Revival,* ed. W. T. Stead and G. Campbell Morgan (Boston: The Pilgrim Press, 1905), 48–63.

THIN PLACES IN IRELAND: THE HILL OF SLANE

In Celtic spirituality, certain locations are known as "thin places"—areas where the veil between the physical and spiritual worlds is considered especially thin. These sites often become powerful landmarks for prayer and spiritual encounters.

One such place is the Hill of Slane in County Meath, Ireland. This hill is where St. Patrick is said to have lit an Easter fire in defiance of the High King, leading to a confrontation that resulted in Patrick's freedom to preach Christianity in Ireland. Today, many Christians visit this site for prayer and reflection, believing it to be a place where heaven and earth draw close together.[33]

The concept of thin places is deeply rooted in Irish Christian tradition. The early Celtic saints often sought out remote and wild places for prayer and communion with God. These locations, often on islands or hilltops, became centers of spiritual activity and pilgrimage. Many believe that in such places the presence of God could be experienced with particular intensity.

Intercessors who pray at these thin places often report a heightened sense of God's presence and

---

[33] "Hill of Slane; The Coming of Christianity," https://www.discoverboynevalley.ie/boyne-valley-drive/heritage-sites/hill-slane-coming-christianity.

a deeper insight into spiritual realities. They use these landmarks as focal points for prayers of national and spiritual significance, much like Daniel praying toward Jerusalem or the early Celtic saints establishing places of prayer.

Challenges in Praying from Landmarks

1. **Avoiding superstition:** Guard against attributing power to the landmark itself rather than God.

2. **Balancing physical and spiritual:** Remember that while landmarks can be significant, God is omnipresent and not limited to specific locations.

3. **Respecting local customs:** When praying at public landmarks, be mindful of local regulations and cultural sensitivities.

4. **Maintaining focus:** Don't let the novelty of the location distract from the purpose of intercession.

Practical Exercise: Landmark Prayer Walk

1. Identify 3–5 significant landmarks in your city or region. These could be historical sites, government buildings, educational institutions, or natural features.

2. Research the history and significance of each landmark.

3. Plan a prayer walk that includes these landmarks. If they're too far apart, consider driving between them.

4. At each landmark:
   - Spend a few minutes in silent reflection, asking God for insights.
   - Pray for the area or institution the landmark represents.
   - Make declarations based on any scriptures or prophetic insights you receive.

5. Journal your experiences and any changes you observe in the following weeks or months.

Conclusion

Praying from landmarks is a powerful tool in prophetic intercession that connects us with God's historical works and future purposes. As we engage in this practice, we participate in a rich biblical tradition and position ourselves as watchmen on the walls (Isa. 62:6). By combining physical location with spiritual insight, we can partner with God in powerful ways to see His will established in our communities and nations.

Remember the words of the prophet Habakkuk: "For the earth will be filled with the knowledge of the glory of the LORD as the waters cover the sea" (Hab. 2:14). As we pray from landmarks, we participate in this glorious filling, calling forth God's purposes from strategic locations across the earth.

CHAPTER 10

HEAVENLY ALLIES: THE ROLE OF ANGELS IN PRAYER

Introduction

Angels play a significant role in the affairs of earth. While they are often misunderstood or sensationalized, Scripture provides clear insights into their nature and function, particularly in relation to prayer and intercession. This chapter explores the biblical foundation for understanding angels, their role in prayer and intercession, and how we can understand angelic activity in our lives as prayer warriors.

Biblical Foundations of Angelic Ministry

OLD TESTAMENT EXAMPLES

- **Jacob's ladder** (Genesis 28:12): "He had a dream in which he saw a stairway resting on the earth, with its top reaching to heaven, and the angels of God were ascending and descending on it."

  This vision illustrates the connection between heaven and earth facilitated by angelic beings.

- **Daniel's angelic encounters** (Daniel 9:20–23): "While I was speaking and praying, confessing my sin and the sin of my people Israel and making my request to the LORD my God for his holy hill—while I was still in prayer, Gabriel, the man I had seen in the earlier vision, came to me in swift flight about the time of the evening sacrifice. He instructed me and said to me, 'Daniel, I have now come to give you insight and understanding. As soon as you began to pray, a word went out, which I have come to tell you, for you are highly esteemed.'"

  This passage below shows an angel bringing answer to prayer and providing insight.

NEW TESTAMENT EXAMPLES

- **Angel announces birth of John** (Luke 1:11–13): An angel was sent to herald the birth of John:

  Then an angel of the Lord appeared to him, standing at the right side of the altar of incense. When Zechariah saw him, he was startled and was gripped with fear. But the angel said to him: "Do not be afraid, Zechariah; your prayer has been heard. Your wife Elizabeth will bear you a son, and you are to call him John."

- **Angels minister to Jesus** (Matthew 4:11): Angels ministered to Jesus after His temptation in the wilderness. "Then the devil left him, and angels came and attended him."

- **Angel delivers Peter from prison** (Acts 12:5–7): An angel was sent in response to the prayer of the church, to release Peter from imprisonment:

  So Peter was kept in prison, but the church was earnestly praying to God for him. The night before Herod was to bring him to trial, Peter was sleeping between two soldiers, bound with two chains, and sentries stood guard at the entrance. Suddenly an angel of the Lord appeared and a light shone in the cell. He struck

Peter on the side and woke him up. "Quick, get up!" he said, and the chains fell off Peter's wrists.

Understanding Angelic Ministry in Prayer and Intercession

Ministering spirits: "Are not all angels ministering spirits sent to serve those who will inherit salvation?" (Heb. 1:14). This verse in Hebrews defines the general role of angels in relation to believers.

Messengers of God: "Praise the Lord, you his angels, you mighty ones who do his bidding, who obey his word" (Ps. 103:20). Angels often serve as messengers, announcing God's word or answers to prayer.

Agents of God's will: Angels are often sent to bring about the will of God in the lives of believers—to deliver them, bring God's healing to them, and guide them.

The angel of the Lord encamps around those
who fear him,
and he delivers them. (Ps. 34:7)

See, I am sending an angel ahead of you to guard you along the way and to bring you to the place I have prepared. Pay attention to him and listen to what he says. Do not rebel against him. (Exod. 23:20–21)

In all their distress he too was distressed, and the angel of his presence saved them. In his love and mercy he redeemed them; he lifted them up and carried them all the days of old. (Isa. 63:9)

Spiritual warfare: Angels are involved in spiritual battles on behalf of believers.

At that time Michael, the great prince who protects your people, will arise. There will be a time of distress such as has not happened from the beginning of nations until then. But at that time your people—everyone whose name is found written in the book—will be delivered. (Dan. 12:1)

Common Misunderstandings About Angels in Prayer

- **Praying to angels**: The biblical model is to pray to God, not to angels directly.
- **Commanding angels**: While believers have authority in Christ, the Bible doesn't instruct us to command angels.
- **Obsession with angelic encounters**: Seeking angelic experiences can distract from focusing on God Himself.
- **Attributing all spiritual experiences to angels**: Not all spiritual experiences or answered prayers necessarily involve direct angelic intervention.
- **Elevating angels Above Christ**: Care must be taken not to elevate angelic ministry above the work of Christ and the Holy Spirit.

Biblical Approach to Aligning with Angelic Activity in Prayer

Focus on God, not angels: Keep the primary focus of prayer on God Himself:

At this I fell at his feet to worship him. But
he said to me, "Don't do that! I am a fellow
servant with you and with your brothers and
sisters who hold to the testimony of Jesus.
Worship God!" (Rev. 19:10)

Pray according to God's will: Align prayers with
God's revealed will in Scripture, which guides
angelic activity:

This is the confidence we have in approaching
God: that if we ask anything according to
his will, he hears us. And if we know that he
hears us—whatever we ask—we know that
we have what we asked of him.
(1 John 5:14–15)

Acknowledge angelic ministry: You can recognize
and thank God for angelic ministry without directly
praying to angels:

For he will command his angels concerning
you to guard you in all your ways; they will
lift you up in their hands, so that you will not
strike your foot against a stone.
(Ps. 91:11–12)

Engage in spiritual warfare: Understand that fervent prayer may activate angelic assistance in spiritual battles:

Then he continued, "Do not be afraid, Daniel. Since the first day that you set your mind to gain understanding and to humble yourself before your God, your words were heard, and I have come in response to them. But the prince of the Persian kingdom resisted me twenty-one days. Then Michael, one of the chief princes, came to help me, because I was detained there with the king of Persia."
(Dan. 10:12–13)

Cultivate awareness of the spiritual realm: Develop sensitivity to the spiritual dimension without seeking sensational experiences.

I pray that the eyes of your heart may be enlightened in order that you may know the hope to which he has called you, the riches of his glorious inheritance in his holy people.
(Eph. 1:18)

> And Elisha prayed, "Open his eyes, LORD,
> so that he may see." Then the LORD opened
> the servant's eyes, and he looked and saw
> the hills full of horses and chariots of fire all
> around Elisha. (2 Kings 6:17)

Modern-Day Examples

ANGEL PROTECTS CHILD FROM TERROR IN THE NIGHT

Dr. Peter Wagner shares a story of seeing an angel in his son's bedroom after he had been waking and screaming in terror during the night. As he prayed to the Lord for help, he asked to see the reality of His angels coming to protect his son:

> Having faith that the Lord would respond to my prayer, I went into little Gonzalo's bedroom. When I opened the door, I was overwhelmed with an awesome force of evil. I felt cold chills. Immediately I sensed the presence of death and knew the Lord was revealing the identity of my enemy.
>
> I sensed the Holy Spirit saying to me, "Take authority in the name of Jesus," and I obeyed. I commanded the spirit of death to get out and never return to torment my son. At that moment,

I saw in my mind a painting of a guardian angel with which I was familiar.

I said, "Lord, You have promised that You would put angels around us for our protection. If it is Your will, I need that protection now, especially for my family." Immediately the bedroom was filled with a brilliant light. I looked toward the crib where Gonzalo was lying, and I saw a huge angel holding a drawn sword. The angel said to me, "From this day on I will be at your son's side to protect him and care for him while you fulfill your divine calling."[34]

PASTOR SURPRISE SITHOLE AND THE ANGEL WITH THE BOW AND ARROW

In his book *Voice in the Night*, Pastor Surprise shares about an angelic encounter in Africa:

All of a sudden, as we zipped along at about seventy miles per hour, I saw a man walking down the middle of the road just ahead of us—a tribesman with a bow and a quiver full of arrows slung over his back. We were headed right for him, but our driver made no attempt to avoid him. "Look out!" I shouted. The driver stamped on the brakes and we squealed to a

---

[34] Wagner, *Breaking Spiritual Strongholds in Your City*, 40.

stop. By the time the car finally came to a rest on the shoulder of the road, we were sprawled all over each other, with Bibles and other materials flung everywhere. After a moment the driver asked, "What? What happened?" "You almost hit him!" I pointed at the tribesman, who was still walking down the middle of the road in the same direction we were heading. "Him, who?" the driver asked. The pastor on my left squinted out of the window and then shook his head. "I don't see anyone." "He's right there!" I pointed again. "Don't you see him?" I could tell from the looks on their faces that they saw nothing…

The man was still there, walking in the same direction we were headed, but we did not get any closer than fifty meters or so. He continued walking ahead of us for some time, until he finally disappeared from view—yet another mystery for me to ponder.[35]

When they finally reached the village they were driving to, a young couple asked him to pray for their young baby who had a high fever and was in a serious condition:

---

[35] Surprise Sithole, *Voice in the Night: The True Story of the Man and Miracles That Are Changing Africa*, (Grand Rapids, MI: Chosen Books, 2012), 117.

I closed my eyes and began to pray. As I did I heard the sound of footsteps behind me. Realizing that someone was coming to join me in prayer, I looked to see who it was—no one was there. I closed my eyes and began to pray a second time. Again I heard the unmistakable sound of the ground crunching beneath someone's feet. I could also feel the presence of someone standing beside me. I looked again— no one there. When this happened a third time, I suddenly realized, Oh—it's the man I saw walking down the middle of the road! My heart was filled with joy because I knew the child would be healed.

Sure enough his fever broke, his eyes opened and he smiled at me. I knew beyond any doubt that God had heard my prayer and that the man I had seen on the road was one of His angels. He had been sent ahead of us to prepare the way for us. Many children were healed and their families saved before our time there was over.[36]

---

[36] Sithole, *Voice in the Night,* 118.

BRUCE VAN NATTA'S NEAR-DEATH EXPERIENCE

Bruce Van Natta, a former atheist turned Christian minister, recounts a life-changing experience following a severe accident:[37]

> I tried to pull myself out from under the truck. It was the most incredible pain you can think of. I got myself just to the point where my head is sticking out from underneath the front bumper of the truck. The very next thing, I just called out, "Lord, help me." I called it out twice.

Instantly, all of the pain left Bruce's body:

> At that point, I became unconscious. My spirit left my body and floated up into the ceiling, and now my spirit is looking at the accident scene from above.
>
> The man I had been working with was on his knees above my body. I can hear him saying things like, "I'm sorry. I'm sorry." But on each side of him, also on their knees were huge angels. If you would have stood them up they would have been about eight feet tall. They did not have wings, just very, very broad shoulders.

---

[37] Bruce Van Natta, "Bruce Van Natta: Saved by Angels," interview with *CBN*, October 12, 2022, https://cbn.com/article/not-selected/bruce-van-natta-saved-angels.

Between the two angels and him, it took up the whole front of this truck.

There was a bright light shining around each one of them. They were matching bookends. They didn't budge; I never heard them say anything. They just had their arms underneath the truck, not holding the truck up . . . but they had their arms angled in toward my body. There was no pain, in fact, just peace. I can't even describe, words can't describe the peace I felt.

Practical Steps for Aligning with Angelic Activity in Prayer

- **Scripture study**: Conduct a thorough study of angelic activity in the Bible to ground your understanding in Scripture.
- **Gratitude practice**: You can regularly thank God for His angelic ministers as part of your prayer life.
- **Kingdom-focused prayers**: Frame your prayers in terms of God's kingdom purposes, which often involve angelic activity.

- **Journaling**: Keep a journal of experiences or answered prayers that may involve angelic activity, always giving glory to God.
- **Intercessory prayer**: Engage in deep intercessory prayer, knowing that such prayer can involve partnering with angelic forces.
- **Worship focus**: Incorporate times of pure worship in your prayer life, and imagine joining with the angelic hosts in glorifying God.

Conclusion

Angels play a significant role in God's interaction with humanity, particularly in the realm of prayer and intercession. While we must be cautious to avoid unbiblical practices or unhealthy fascination with angels, we can benefit greatly from a biblical understanding of their ministry. By aligning our prayers with God's purposes and maintaining a focus on Christ, we open ourselves to the full spectrum of divine assistance, including the ministry of angels. Remember, the goal is not to seek angelic experiences, but to fully engage in God's kingdom purposes, in which angels play a vital supportive role.

Part III

DIVING DEEPER: DEEPENING THE PRACTICE

CHAPTER 11

LABOR PAINS IN THE SPIRIT: TRAVAILING IN PRAYER FOR GOD'S PURPOSES

Introduction

Certain experiences of prophetic intercession carry a depth of prayer so intense that they are often likened to the process of childbirth. This is known as travailing prayer. Far from being a mere emotional display, travailing in prayer is a biblical concept that speaks to the heart of partnering with God to bring His purposes to fruition. This chapter explores the scriptural foundations of travailing prayer, its significance in both biblical and modern times, and how we can engage in this powerful form of intercession.

Josh Green, youth director for 24-7 Prayer and Wildfire Youth in Manchester, England says "Travailing prayer, then, is from deep longing within the soul and can often be a painful, birth-like experience. It's a true expression of allowing God to break our hearts for what breaks His. This is prayer that doesn't expect to move God if it doesn't first move the human heart."[38]

Biblical Foundations of Travailing Prayer

OLD TESTAMENT EXAMPLES

- **Hannah's prayer for a son** (1 Samuel 1:10–17): "In her deep anguish Hannah prayed to the LORD, weeping bitterly" (v. 10). Hannah's intense, tearful prayer for a child exemplifies travailing prayer.

- **Moses interceding for Israel** (Exodus 32:32): "But now, please forgive their sin—but if not, then blot me out of the book you have written." Moses' willingness to be blotted out for the sake of Israel shows the depth of travailing intercession.

---

[38] Josh Green, "The Call to Desperate Intercession: What is Travailing Prayer?" *24-7 Prayer,* accessed September 20, 2024, https://www.24-7prayer.com/the-call-to-desperate-intercession-what-is-travailing-prayer/.

- **David's repentance** (Psalm 51): "My sacrifice, O God, is a broken spirit; a broken and contrite heart you, God, will not despise" (Psalm 51:17). David's deep anguish over his sin reflects a form of travailing prayer.

NEW TESTAMENT EXAMPLES

- **Jesus in Gethsemane** (Luke 22:44): "And being in anguish, he prayed more earnestly, and his sweat was like drops of blood falling to the ground." Jesus' intense prayer before His crucifixion is a profound example of travailing.

- **Paul's burden for the church** (Galatians 4:19): "My dear children, for whom I am again in the pains of childbirth until Christ is formed in you . . ." Paul uses the metaphor of childbirth to describe his intense prayer for spiritual growth in believers.

- **The Holy Spirit's intercession** (Romans 8:26–27): "In the same way, the Spirit helps us in our weakness. We do not know what we ought to pray for, but the Spirit himself intercedes for us through wordless groans. And he who searches our hearts knows the mind of the Spirit, because the Spirit intercedes for God's people in accordance with the will of God."

The Holy Spirit's groaning intercession aligns with the concept of travailing prayer.

Understanding Travailing Prayer

- **Spiritual birth pangs:** Just as physical birth involves labor, so too, travailing prayer involves spiritual labor to birth God's purposes.
- **Depth of burden:** Travailing prayer reflects a deep, often painful, burden for God's will to be accomplished.
- **Persistence and intensity**: It involves praying with a level of intensity and persistence that goes beyond routine prayer.
- **Partnership with God:** Travailing prayer is a form of partnering with God to bring His plans to fruition.
- **Power:** This type of prayer often leads to significant breakthroughs and transformations.

Insights from Prayer Warriors

To further describe the concept and importance of travailing prayer, consider these powerful quotes from various Christian leaders and authors:

Dr. Michael Yeager, in his book *Travailing in Prayer: Understanding Intercessory Prayer*, shares a vivid description of travailing prayer:

> Just as a woman endures immense pain during childbirth, sometimes to the point of risking her life, so too does travailing in the Spirit involve a kind of spiritual agony. It's a process where you feel like you're dying, metaphorically, out of love for those you are praying for. This experience is not just about self-sacrifice; it's about partaking in the profound agony of spiritual birth.[39]

E. M. Bounds, 19th-century pastor and author known for his works on prayer, records the lessons of travailing prayer he gleaned from earlier examples of Christian ministry. For instance, he cites Adoniram Judson:

> A travailing spirit, the throes of a great burdened desire, belongs to prayer. A fervency strong enough to drive away sleep, which devotes and inflames the spirit, and which retires all earthly ties, all this belongs to wrestling, prevailing

---

[39] Michael Yeager, *Travailing in Prayer: Understanding Intercessory Prayer* (self-pub: Michael H. Yeager, 2023), 53.

prayer. The Spirit, the power, the air, and food of prayer is in such a spirit.[40]

And when describing the ministry of David Brainerd, he cites Jonathan Edwards:

Animated with love to Christ and souls, how did he labor? Always fervently. Not only in word and doctrine, in public and in private, but in prayers by day and night, wrestling with God in secret and travailing in birth with unutterable groans and agonies, until Christ was formed in the hearts of the people to whom he was sent. Like a true son of Jacob, he persevered in wrestling through all the darkness of the night, until the breaking of the day![41]

John Dawson, author of *Taking Our Cities for God*, tells us:

There are times when God's Spirit stirs our souls to seasons of intense travail. We must travail in prayer until God's purposes are birthed. This may be an exercise that is deeply personal and private or a corporate exercise, for example, as part of scheduled citywide prayer meetings. That which is conceived of God will eventually

---

[40] E. M. Bounds, *The Complete Works of E. M. Bounds on Prayer: Experience the Wonders of God through Prayer* (Grand Rapids, MI: Baker Books, 1990), 37.

[41] Bounds, *The Complete Works,* 470.

come to birth. When the united Christians of a city are at this stage, it is an indicator of impending revival.[42]

Leonard Ravenhill, author and evangelist, writes:

No man is greater than his prayer life. The pastor who is not praying is playing; the people who are not praying are straying. . . . We have many organizers, but few agonizers; many players and payers, few pray-ers; many singers, few clingers; lots of pastors, few wrestlers; many fears, few tears; much fashion, little passion; many interferers, few intercessors; many writers, but few fighters. Failing here, we fail everywhere.[43]

Chuck Pierce tells us that "there is tremendous power in travailing prayer because it births the will of God on Earth. This type of prayer always outflanks the devil, who is so strongly opposed by the new thing God is producing as a result of travail."[44]

---

[42] John Dawson, *Taking Our Cities for God* (Lake Mary, FL: Charisma House, 2001), 160.

[43] Leonard Ravenhill, *Why Revival Tarries* (Minneapolis: Bethany House Publishers, 1987), 25.

[44] Chuck D. Pierce, *The Future War of the Church* (Ventura, CA: Regal Books, 2001), 151.

Cindy Jacobs, too, likens travailing prayer to "experiencing the pangs of childbirth" on behalf of a person or place in order to "help to birth the will of God into that area."[45] She explains:

> There will be times when we are interceding that we seem to feel or identify with the sorrow of the person for whom we are praying, or we will know the grieving of the Holy Spirit over a person's sin. When we enter into this kind of prayer, we will experience manifestations such as travailing, weeping and laughing. Sometimes these strong emotions take the intercessor quite by surprise. They cannot be forced to occur—it is as the Spirit wills.[46]

These insights from experienced intercessors highlight the depth, intensity, and power of travailing prayer. They underscore that this form of intercession goes beyond routine prayer, involving a deep partnership with God's heart and purposes.

Characteristics of Travailing Prayer

- **Emotional intensity:** May involve weeping, groaning, or other expressions of deep emotion.

---

[45] Cindy Jacobs, *Possessing the Gates of the Enemy: A Training Manual for Militant Intercession* (Grand Rapids, MI: Chosen Books, 1991), 115.

[46] Jacobs, *Possessing the Gates*, 112.

- **Physical manifestations:** Can be physically demanding, as seen in Jesus' prayer in Gethsemane.

- **Spiritual discernment:** Often involves a deep, Spirit-led understanding of what to pray for.

- **Sacrificial nature:** May involve personal sacrifice or discomfort for the sake of the prayer burden.

- **Focused persistence:** Characterized by a refusal to give up until the "birth" occurs.

Modern-Day Example

LOU ENGLE AND THE CALL

Lou Engle, known for mobilizing prayer movements, often speaks of travailing prayer. He shares:

> During a period of extended fasting in prayer in 1986 I was reimmersing myself in the history of this powerful, transforming work of God [the Azuza revival]. Eighteen days into my fast, the burden for revival came upon me so strongly one night that I began to cry aloud. . . . I was arrested by a spirit of travail and called out fervently to the Lord late into the night.[47]

---

[47] Lou Engle and Dean Briggs, *The Jesus Fast: The Call to Awaken the Nations* (Minneapolis: Chosen Books, 2016), Kindle location 38.

Practical Exercises and Activations

- **Burden identification:** Spend time in quiet reflection, asking God to reveal specific burdens He wants you to travail in prayer for.
- **Prayer vigil:** Set aside an extended time (e.g., 3–6 hours) for focused, intense prayer on a specific issue, allowing yourself to enter into travail as led by the Spirit.
- **Intercessory journaling:** As you pray, write down any impressions, scriptures, or burdens you feel. This can help you track the "labor process" of your travailing prayer.
- **Physical prayer:** Engage your body in prayer through kneeling, pacing, or lying prostrate. Allow physical postures to reinforce your spiritual intensity.
- **Group travail:** Gather with other intercessors to travail in prayer together, supporting one another through the intensity of the experience.

A Word of Caution: Balancing Intensity and Self-Care

While travailing prayer can be a powerful spiritual practice, it's crucial to approach it with wisdom and care. The intensity of this form of intercession can potentially lead to emotional exhaustion or burnout if not balanced with proper self-care and spiritual discernment.

Biblical Perspective on Balance

Rest after intensity: After Elijah's intense spiritual battle on Mount Carmel, he experienced exhaustion and depression. God's response was to provide rest and nourishment:

[Elijah] went a day's journey into the wilderness. He came to a broom bush, sat down under it and prayed that he might die. 'I have had enough, LORD,' he said. 'Take my life; I am no better than my ancestors.' Then he lay down under the bush and fell asleep. All at once an angel touched him and said, 'Get up and eat.' He looked around, and there by his head was some bread baked over hot coals, and a jar of water. He ate and drank and then lay down again. (1 Kings 19:4–8)

Jesus' example of solitary withdrawal: Jesus modeled the importance of balancing intense ministry with times of solitude and rest, as Luke

5:16 tells us: *"But Jesus often withdrew to lonely places and prayed."*

Practical Wisdom for Self-Care

- **Set boundaries:** Establish time limits for intense prayer sessions and honor them as you are learning.
- **Practice debriefing:** After intense prayer times, take time to process your experiences, perhaps through journaling or talking with a trusted spiritual mentor.
- **Embrace the sabbath:** Regular times of rest and renewal are crucial for sustainable prayer ministry.
- **Physical care:** Pay attention to your body's needs for sleep, nutrition, and exercise.
- **Community support:** Share the burden of travailing prayer with others rather than carrying it alone.
- **Be self-aware:** Are you praying in your own strength? Sometimes we don't realize we fall into works and out of that place of rest that the Father wants us to live from.

- **Celebrate and rest:** After periods of travail, take time to celebrate breakthroughs and rest in God's presence.

Remember, even Jesus, who travailed intensely in prayer, also enjoyed times of celebration and rest. (Think of Jesus at the wedding in Cana in John 2:1–11.) As we engage in travailing prayer, let's do so with wisdom, balance, and an awareness of our human limitations, trusting in God's strength rather than our own.

Conclusion

Travailing prayer is not for the faint of heart, but for those willing to partner deeply with God's purposes. It's a form of intercession that goes beyond casual requests, tapping into the very heart of God for situations, people, and nations. As we learn to engage in travailing prayer, we position ourselves to see significant breakthroughs and to participate in birthing God's will on earth as it is in heaven.

CHAPTER 12

HUNGER FOR BREAKTHROUGH: FASTING AND INTERCESSION

Introduction

*f*asting has long been recognized as a powerful spiritual discipline that can heighten our sensitivity to God's voice and intensify our prayers. When combined with intercession, fasting can lead to breakthrough experiences and deeper spiritual insights. Certain evil spirits, Jesus said, do "not go out except by prayer and fasting" (Matt. 17:21). Such statements should make us consider fasting as an effective weapon in our prayer tool belt.

Biblical Foundations of Fasting and Intercession

OLD TESTAMENT EXAMPLES

- **Moses' experience:** Exodus 34:28 describes how Moses fasted for 40 days and nights while receiving the Ten Commandments: "Moses was there with the LORD forty days and forty nights without eating bread or drinking water. And he wrote on the tablets the words of the covenant—the Ten Commandments."

- **Daniel's revelation:** In Daniel 10:2–3, we see Daniel engaging in a partial fast for three weeks before receiving a significant prophetic vision: "At that time I, Daniel, mourned for three weeks. I ate no choice food; no meat or wine touched my lips; and I used no lotions at all until the three weeks were over."

- **Esther's intervention:** Esther 4:16 shows Esther calling for a fast before her crucial intervention for her people: "Go, gather together all the Jews who are in Susa, and fast for me. Do not eat or drink for three days, night or day. I and my attendants will fast as you do. When this is done, I will go to the king, even though it is against the law. And if I perish, I perish."

NEW TESTAMENT TEACHINGS

- **Jesus' teaching**: In Matthew 6:16–18, Jesus assumes His followers will fast, providing instructions on how to do so with the right heart:

"When you fast, do not look somber as the hypocrites do, for they disfigure their faces to show others they are fasting. Truly I tell you, they have received their reward in full. But when you fast, put oil on your head and wash your face, so that it will not be obvious to others that you are fasting, but only to your Father, who is unseen; and your Father, who sees what is done in secret, will reward you."

- **Fasting to appoint God-chosen ministers**: In Acts 13:2–3 14:23 describe how early ministers and missionaries in the church were chosen during times of intense prayer and fasting.

The Purpose of Fasting in Intercession

Fasting serves several purposes in enhancing prophetic intercession:

1. **Heightened spiritual sensitivity**: Fasting can help quiet physical distractions, making us more attuned to God's voice.

2. **Humility and dependence**: Fasting reminds us of our dependence on God, fostering a humble and receptive spirit.

3. **Intensified prayer**: Fasting often leads to more focused and passionate prayer.

4. **Spiritual warfare**: Fasting can be a powerful weapon in spiritual battles, as indicated by Jesus' words in Mark 9:29.

5. **Clarity and direction**: Fasting can help clear our minds and hearts, allowing for clearer direction from God.

Types of Fasts

There are many ways you can fast, here are a few ideas:

1. **Complete fast**: Abstaining from all food and drink except water.

2. **Partial fast**: Restricting certain foods or eating only at certain times.

3. **Daniel fast**: Based on Daniel's example, typically avoiding meat, sweets, and processed foods.

4. **Media fast**: Abstaining from various forms of media to focus on prayer.
5. **Corporate fast**: Fasting as a community or church body.

Practical Guidelines for Fasting

1. **Start small**: If you're new to fasting, start with shorter fasts and work your way up.
2. **Stay hydrated**: Always drink plenty of water during a fast.
3. **Plan your prayer time**: Use the time you would normally spend eating for focused prayer and Bible study.
4. **Break the fast gradually**: Especially for longer fasts, ease back into normal eating.
5. **Consider health conditions**: Consult a doctor if you have any health concerns before starting a fast.

Real-life Examples of Fasting and Intercession

THE WELSH REVIVAL OF 1904

One of the most powerful examples of the impact of fasting and intercession comes from the Welsh

Revival of 1904. Evan Roberts, a young coal miner turned seminary student, felt led by God to return to his home church in Moriah Loughor, Wales. For months, Roberts had been praying for revival, often spending hours in prayer and fasting.[48]

On October 31, 1904, Roberts shared a vision he had received with young people at a church meeting. He encouraged them to pray a simple prayer: "Send the Spirit now, for Jesus Christ's sake."[49] The group prayed until 2 a.m., and the revival began. Over the next few months, over 100,000 people came to faith in Wales.

Evan Roberts later said: "This movement is not of me; it is of God. I would not dare direct it. Obey the Spirit, that is our word in everything. It is the Spirit alone which is leading us in our meetings and in all that is done."[50]

This revival, which spread to other parts of the world, was preceded by intense periods of prayer

---

[48] Dennis Pollock, "Evan Roberts & the Welsh Revival," *Spirit of Grace Ministries,* accessed September 12, 2024, https://www.spiritofgrace.org/articles/nl_2014/extras/00_evan_roberts.html.

[49] Evan Roberts, "Keys for Revival," *The Revival Library,* accessed September 12, 2024, https://revival-library.org/revival-resources/for-revival-seekers/revival-tips-from-history/evan-roberts-keys-of-revival/.

[50] Tony Cauchi, "Evan Roberts and War on the Saints," *Sermonindex,* November 2007, https://www.sermonindex.net/modules/newbb/viewtopic.php?topic_id=32414&forum=40.

and fasting, not just by Roberts but by many others who had been seeking God for a spiritual awakening.

HEIDI BAKER'S MINISTRY IN MOZAMBIQUE

Heidi Baker, a missionary in Mozambique, shares how fasting has been crucial in her ministry among the poor and in seeing miraculous healings and provision.[51] She often engages in extended fasts, seeking God's direction and breakthrough. Heidi writes:

"Do you love him more than your schedule? Do you love him more than being connected with people? More than food? More than comfort? It's not that we are never going to have those beautiful blessings. It's just that he knows why, and he knows how he wants to call you to fast. When he is leading, fasting actually becomes a delight. This is what I am discovering for myself. Fasting time, when I don't meet with anybody and I just meet with him, has been some of the most powerful and precious fasting ever."[52]

---

[51] Heidi Baker, "Fasting," Facebook, September 6, 2019, https://www.facebook.com/photo. php?fbid=2630797913610570&id=170111516345901&set=a.498038696886513.

[52] Heidi Baker and Jennifer Miscov, "Jesus Said, 'Come into the Desert with Me,'" *Destiny Image,* accessed September 20, 2024, https://www.destinyimage.com/blog/heidi-baker-jennifer-miskov-come-into-the-desert-with-me.

Heidi attributes many miracles to these times of focused fasting and intercession.

Challenges in Fasting

1. **Physical discomfort**: Hunger, headaches, and fatigue are common, especially in the beginning.
2. **Spiritual warfare**: Increased spiritual opposition can occur during fasts.
3. **Discouragement**: Lack of immediate results can be discouraging.
4. **Legalism**: Avoid turning fasting into a legalistic practice rather than a heart-centered one.

Integrating Fasting with Prophetic Intercession

1. **Set clear intentions**: Begin your fast with clear prayer objectives.
2. **Journal insights**: Record any prophetic insights or scriptures you receive during your fast.
3. **Combine with worship**: Incorporate worship into your fasting periods to enhance your spiritual focus.

4. **Community fasting**: Consider fasting with others for mutual encouragement and increased spiritual power.

5. **Follow-up action**: Be prepared to act on the insights and direction you receive during your fast.

Conclusion

Fasting, when combined with prophetic intercession, can be a catalyst for personal and corporate spiritual breakthrough. It intensifies our prayers, sharpens our spiritual senses, and deepens our dependence on God.

> "Is not this the kind of fasting I have chosen: to loose the chains of injustice and untie the cords of the yoke, to set the oppressed free and break every yoke?" (Isaiah 58:6)

Let your fasting not just be about personal spiritual growth, but about seeing God's kingdom come and His will be done on earth as it is in heaven. As you fast and intercede, may you experience new depths of God's presence and power in your prayers.

CORPORATE PROPHETIC INTERCESSION: UNITING FOR WAR

Introduction

Corporate prophetic intercession is a powerful form of prayer where a group of believers come together to seek God's heart and pray His will into existence. It combines the strength of unity with the insight of prophecy, creating a formidable spiritual force. As Jesus said, "For where two or three gather in my name, there am I with them" (Matthew 18:20).

Biblical Foundations of Corporate Intercession

1. **Perseverance in communal prayer**: Acts 1:14 describes the first moment of the early church,

awaiting the outpouring of the Holy Spirit at Pentecost: "They all joined together constantly in prayer."

2. **Corporate seeking**: In 2 Chronicles 20, King Jehoshaphat faced a vast army. His response was to call a fast and gather the people to seek the Lord together. Similarly, in Esther 4, when the Jewish nation was threatened with extermination during the captivity in Babylon, Esther called upon all the Jews to fast on her behalf before she approached the king.

3. **Agreement in prayer**: Jesus taught in Matthew 18:19, "Again, truly I tell you that if two of you on earth agree about anything they ask for, it will be done for them by my Father in heaven."

4. **Prophetic element**: In Acts 13:1–3, we see the church at Antioch fasting and praying together when the Holy Spirit spoke, directing them to send out Barnabas and Saul.

The Power of Corporate Prophetic Intercession

Seasoned intercessor Mahesh Chavda speaks powerfully of the importance of corporate prayer in the church, saying that "Christ's call to His Church today is for corporate prayer—intimate communion with Him and intercession that moves heaven and earth for the purposes of God."[53]

He goes on to say the following in different portions of his book *The Hidden Power of Speaking in Tongues:*

> "In terms of our lives as disciples of Christ, prayer is where everything begins and ends. Nothing God wills to do on earth will happen without prayer. On the other hand, when believers pray, particularly in concert with one another, nothing is impossible. Jesus said, "If two of you agree on earth concerning anything that they ask, it will be done for them by My Father in heaven. For where two or three are gathered together in My name, I am there in the midst of them" (Mt. 18:19–0). What an awesome promise this is! Do we truly comprehend the magnitude of what is available to us? Other than the Lord Himself, no power or principality in either the natural or spiritual realms can match the power of His people united in corporate prayer."[54]

> "Corporate prayer is our greatest weapon against the spirit of antichrist. The powers of

---

[53] Chavda, *The Hidden Power of Speaking in Tongues*, 181.

[54] Chavda, *The Hidden Power of Speaking in Tongues*, 180.

darkness cannot stand against the assault of God's people praying with one accord in the power and anointing of the Spirit."[55]

"We say we want to be where God is. Well, God is where prayer is, and He is especially present in the environment of corporate prayer. A body of committed believers praying in harmony together in the Spirit connect with the glory of God and create an atmosphere in which He is pleased to dwell."[56]

Key Elements of Corporate Prophetic Intercession

1. **Unity of purpose**: All participants should be aligned in their focus and intent.
2. **Sensitivity to the Holy Spirit**: The group must be attuned to God's leading and open to prophetic insights.
3. **Structured leadership**: While allowing for spontaneity, having designated leadership helps maintain focus and order.

---

[55] Chavda, *The Hidden Power of Speaking in Tongues*, 182.
[56] Chavda, *The Hidden Power of Speaking in Tongues*, 183.

4. **Scriptural foundation**: All prophetic insights and prayers should be grounded in and aligned with Scripture.

5. **Discernment**: The group should practice discernment, testing every word or impression against Scripture and the witness of other mature believers.

Practical Steps for Corporate Prophetic Intercession

1. **Prepare**: Encourage participants to come having spent time in personal prayer and Scripture reading.

2. **Set the atmosphere**: Begin with worship to focus hearts on God.

3. **Establish the focus**: Clearly communicate the prayer focus for the session.

4. **Listen together**: Spend time in silent listening, allowing God to speak to the group.

5. **Share insights**: Allow time for individuals to share what they believe God is saying.

6. **Pray in agreement**: Based on the shared insights, pray together in agreement.

7. **Record**: Designate someone to record the prophetic insights and prayers for future reference and follow-up.

Overcoming Challenges in Corporate Prophetic Intercession

1. **Distractions:** Maintain focus through gentle reminders and redirecting prayer.
2. **Domination by individuals:** Ensure everyone has the opportunity to participate.
3. **Discerning true prophecy:** Establish guidelines for sharing prophetic insights and teach the group to discern. For example, make sure your process aligns with Scripture, the lifestyle of the person giving the prophecy is godly, and their track record of accuracy is good.
4. **Maintaining unity:** Address disagreements with love and always prioritize unity.

A Powerful Example: The Cali Prayer Movement

One remarkable example of corporate prophetic intercession comes from Cali, Colombia, in the

1990s.[57] The city was known as the drug and crime capital of Colombia. In 1995, a group of pastors and intercessors felt led by God to organize a stadium prayer gathering.

The event, which they thought might draw 5,000 people, attracted over 25,000. During the gathering, there were numerous prophetic words about God cleansing the city and bringing transformation. The group engaged in intense, unified prayer based on these prophetic insights.

In the months and years that followed, Cali saw a dramatic decrease in crime rates, drug trafficking, and corruption. Many attributed this transformation to the power of corporate prophetic intercession.

Cultivating a Culture of Corporate Prophetic Intercession

1. **Regular gatherings:** Establish consistent times for corporate prayer.
2. **Training**: Provide teaching on both prophecy and intercession.
3. **Accountability**: Create a system for following up on prophetic words and prayers.

---

[57] Chet & Phyllis Swearingen, "1995 Cali, Colombia Revival," *Beautiful Feet,* accessed September 12, 2024, https://romans1015.com/cali/.

4. **Celebration**: Regularly share testimonies of answered prayers to build faith.
5. **Community building**: Foster relationships among intercessors outside of prayer times.

Conclusion

Corporate prophetic intercession is a powerful tool in the hands of the church. When believers come together in unity, seeking God's heart and praying His will into existence, remarkable things can happen. As you engage in this practice, remember the words popularly attributed to Charles Spurgeon: "Prayer meetings are the throbbing machinery of the church."

May your times of corporate prophetic intercession be marked by unity, power, and the clear leading of the Holy Spirit, resulting in transformation in your communities and beyond.

CHAPTER 14

NATIONS IN THE BALANCE: INTERCEDING FOR LANDS AND LEADERS

Introduction

Prophetic intercession for nations and leaders is a vital ministry that can shape the destiny of entire peoples and influence global events. As we engage in this level of intercession, we partner with God in His purposes for the nations, as stated in Psalm 2:8: "Ask me, and I will make the nations your inheritance, the ends of the earth your possession."

Biblical Foundations

OLD TESTAMENT EXAMPLES

- **Abraham's intercession:** In Genesis 18, Abraham intercedes for Sodom, negotiating with God for the sake of the righteous in the city.

- **Jeremiah's call:** In Jeremiah 1:10, God says, "See, today I appoint you over nations and kingdoms to uproot and tear down, to destroy and overthrow, to build and to plant." This demonstrates the spiritual authority given to prophetic intercessors.

- **Daniel's intercession:** Daniel 9 shows Daniel interceding for his nation based on prophetic insights from Jeremiah's writings.

NEW TESTAMENT TEACHING

- **Paul's instruction:** 1 Timothy 2:1–2 encourages, "I urge, then, first of all, that petitions, prayers, intercession and thanksgiving be made for all people—for kings and all those in authority."

Key Principles in Interceding for Nations and Leaders

1. **Seek God's heart**: Before interceding, spend time seeking God's perspective on the nation or leader.
2. **Use Scripture**: Base your prayers on biblical principles and promises related to governance and nations.
3. **Pray with authority**: Recognize the spiritual authority given to believers in Christ.
4. **Be specific**: Address specific issues, policies, and decisions facing nations and leaders.
5. **Persistence**: Nations and governments often require sustained intercession over time.
6. **Discernment**: Be attentive to prophetic insights that can guide your prayers.
7. **Bless, don't curse**: Even when praying about corrupt leaders, focus on God's redemptive purposes.

Practical Steps in Prophetic Intercession for Nations

1. **Research**: Gather factual information about the nation's history, culture, and current issues. (I highly recommend *Operation World: The*

Definitive Prayer Guide to Every Nation by Jason Mandryk).[58]

2. **Identify key areas**: Focus on government, economy, education, media, arts and entertainment, family, and religion, as well as whatever in particular might constitute the sins against God in that nation.[59]

3. **Listen prophetically**: Spend time listening for God's heart and specific directives for the nation.

4. **Declare God's purposes**: Make faith-filled declarations based on Scripture and prophetic insights.

5. **Engage in spiritual warfare**: Recognize and address spiritual strongholds over nations.

6. **Involve others**: Organize or join groups focused on intercession for nations and leaders.

Real-life Examples

TRANSFORMATION IN GUATEMALA

In the early 1980s, Guatemala was suffering from a brutal civil war and economic crisis. A group of intercessors began focused prayer for the nation.

---

[58] Jason Mandryk, *Operation World: The Definitive Prayer Guide to Every Nation*, 7th ed. (Crown Hill, UK: Authentic Media, 2010).

[59] Jacobs, *Possessing the Gates*, 236–38.

They reported receiving prophetic insights about God's plans to transform Guatemala.

Over the next two decades, sustained intercession and strategic prayer initiatives coincided with significant positive changes in the nation. The civil war ended, democratic processes strengthened, and there was notable economic improvement. Many attributed these changes to the power of what we would call prophetic intercession.[60]

THE FALL OF THE BERLIN WALL

Prior to the fall of the Berlin Wall in 1989, there was a significant prayer movement in East Germany. Christian Führer, a pastor in Leipzig, organized weekly prayer meetings that grew into peaceful demonstrations.

Führer later stated, "We brought the candles and the prayers out of the church into the streets."[61] Many believe these prayer initiatives, which included prophetic declarations of freedom and unity, played a crucial role in the peaceful revolution that led to the fall of the Berlin Wall.

---

[60] An example of such transformation is the wholesale conversion of Almolonga, Guatemala. See George Otis, Jr., "Snapshots of Glory," *Renewal Journal* 17, 12 September 2011, https://renewaljournal.com/2011/09/12/snapshots-of-glory-bygeorge-otis-jr/.

[61] Christian Führer, "Voices of a Revolution: Leipzig," *NPR*, November 9, 2009, https://www.npr.org/2009/11/09/120251039/voices-of-a-revolution-leipzig.

Challenges in Interceding for Nations and Leaders

1. **Avoiding political bias**: Stay focused on God's purposes rather than personal political preferences.

2. **Handling sensitive information**: Exercise wisdom with any sensitive prophetic insights about leaders or nations.

3. **Maintaining hope**: When change is slow, it can be discouraging. Remember that God's timelines often differ from ours.

4. **Spiritual warfare**: Intercession at this level can invite spiritual opposition. Stay vigilant and grounded in Scripture.

I love what Cindy Jacobs says: "Your prayers are weapons shaping history in times of war."[62] When we pray for nations, we don't just change decisions or circumstances, we are literally partnering with the Lord to shape the destiny of that nation.

---

[62] Cindy Jacobs, "Your Prayers are Weapons Shaping History in Times of War," YouTube, November 19, 2023, https://youtu.be/VqRU6S9OC_g?si=Lenj3EudZLdUPG_N.

Practical Exercise: Prophetic Intercession for a Nation

1. Choose a nation to focus on.
2. Spend time in worship and listening prayer, asking God for His heart for this nation.
3. Research the nation's current situation, leadership, and pressing issues.
4. Write down any scriptures, visions, or impressions you receive.
5. Formulate specific prayers and declarations based on your research and prophetic insights.
6. Commit to praying for this nation regularly over a set period (e.g., 30 days).
7. Journal any changes you observe or further insights you receive during this time.

Conclusion

Prophetic intercession for nations and leaders is a high calling that requires dedication, discernment, and a deep reliance on the Holy Spirit. As you engage in this level of intercession, I am reminded of 2 Chronicles 7:14:

"If my people, who are called by my name, will humble themselves and pray and seek my face and turn from their wicked ways, then I will hear from heaven, and I will forgive their sin and will heal their land."

Your prayers have the power to influence the course of nations and the decisions of leaders. As you faithfully intercede, trust that God is working, often in ways we cannot immediately see, to bring His purposes to pass in the nations of the earth. In the words of Mahesh Chavda: "It is time for us to man our posts, repair the breaches, and close the wall of intercession surrounding the nations."[63]

---

[63] Chavda, *The Hidden Power of Speaking in Tongues*, 183.

Part IV

NAVIGATING STORMY SEAS: OVERCOMING CHALLENGES IN INTERCESSION

CHAPTER 15

FORTIFYING THE WATCHTOWERS: SPIRITUAL PROTECTION FOR INTERCESSORS

Introduction

As intercessors step into the gap on behalf of others, they often find themselves on the front lines of spiritual warfare. This heightened spiritual activity can sometimes lead to various forms of attack, including spiritual oppression and even physical illness. This chapter explores biblical principles and practical strategies for maintaining spiritual protection while engaging in deep intercessory prayer.

Biblical Foundations of Spiritual Protection

OLD TESTAMENT EXAMPLES

- **Daniel's protection in prayer** (Daniel 6:10–23): Despite the threat of death, Daniel continued his prayer routine, and God protected him in the lions' den.

- **Elisha's spiritual sight** (2 Kings 6:15–17): "And Elisha prayed, *'Open his eyes, LORD, so that he may see.'* Then the LORD opened the servant's eyes, and he looked and saw the hills full of horses and chariots of fire all around Elisha" (v. 17). This passage illustrates the unseen spiritual protection surrounding God's servants.

- **Nehemiah's vigilance** (Nehemiah 4:9): "But we prayed to our God and posted a guard day and night to meet this threat." Nehemiah combined prayer with practical protective measures.

NEW TESTAMENT TEACHINGS

- **The armor of God** (Ephesians 6:10–18): Paul's detailed description of spiritual armor provides a framework for protection in spiritual warfare.

It would be beneficial for you to do a deep-dive study on this armor and make sure there are no places of weakness in your life where the enemy could attack you. Is there any part of this spiritual armor that you need to work on in your life?

- **The power of the name of Jesus** (Philippians 2:9–10): "Therefore God exalted him to the highest place and gave him the name that is above every name, that at the name of Jesus every knee should bow, in heaven and on earth and under the earth."

- **Resistance and firm faith** (1 Peter 5:8–9): "Be alert and of sober mind. Your enemy the devil prowls around like a roaring lion looking for someone to devour. Resist him, standing firm in the faith."

Understanding Spiritual Attacks on Intercessors

If you commit to pray in a way that can bring Heaven to Earth, you are a threat to the enemy's plans. He will do all he can to stop you from praying. Here are some attacks that may come against you. I am sharing this to help you notice that they are attacks so that you are not deceived and can stand strong in the Lord.

1. **Heightened spiritual activity:** Intercession often brings intercessors into direct conflict with spiritual forces opposing God's will.

2. **Physical manifestations:** Spiritual attacks can sometimes manifest as physical symptoms or illnesses.

3. **Mental and emotional pressure:** Intercessors may experience increased fear, doubt, or discouragement.

4. **Relational strain:** Attacks may come through conflicts in relationships or increased isolation.

5. **Intensified temptation:** Intercessors might face stronger temptations in areas of personal weakness.

Strategies for Spiritual Protection

1. **Put on the full armor of God:** Each piece of spiritual armor described in Ephesians 6 is important to God. Is there anything you are not putting into practice in your life that might cause you to have a weak spot where the enemy can get in?

2. **Maintain strong boundaries:** Set clear spiritual and emotional boundaries in your intercessory ministry.

3. **Practice regular self-care:** Balance intense prayer times with rest, worship, and personal refreshment.

4. **Stay accountable:** Maintain close relationships with mature believers who can provide support and discernment.

5. **Prayer protection:** Ask for the prayers of fellow believers, especially in moments of more intense intercession. Paul assures the Colossians that they have a strong defense in Epaphras: "He is always wrestling in prayer for you, that you may stand firm in all the will of God, mature and fully assured" (Col. 4:12).

6. **The name of Jesus:** There is Power in the Name of Jesus! His name carries authority over all spiritual forces. Say His name and pray in His name!

"And these signs will accompany those who believe: In my name they will drive out demons; they will speak in new tongues; they will pick up snakes with their hands; and when they drink deadly poison, it will not

hurt them at all; they will place their hands
on sick people, and they will get well." (Mark
16:17–18)

7. **Cultivate spiritual discernment:** Develop
   sensitivity to the Holy Spirit's guidance and
   warnings. Sometimes when we are passionate
   about what we are praying for we do not discern
   the danger and do not pray accordingly.

8. **Declare Scripture:** There is nothing better
   than knowing the Word of God. When we
   know the scriptures, we can use it like a sword
   and speak it out and declare it. When we do
   this, it's like a shield against spiritual attacks.

   Jesus demonstrated the power of declaring
   Scripture when He was tempted in the
   wilderness (Matt. 4:3–11). This strategy is
   powerfully illustrated in Ephesians 6:17: "Take
   the helmet of salvation and the sword of the
   Spirit, which is the word of God."

   These verses emphasize that God's word is both
   offensive (a sword) and defensive (a shield) in
   spiritual warfare, making it an essential tool for
   intercessors seeking protection.

Insights from Experienced Intercessors

James Goll: "The Old Testament picture from the life of Gideon gives us insight into the necessity of praying a hedge of protection around ourselves and our families, and breaking, in the name of Jesus, any curse or penalty that the enemy tries to enforce on God's people when they are confronting darkness. After engaging in a power encounter with the enemy, I have learned from experience to offer up a prayer breaking any possible counterattack that the enemy would release against me. This includes attacks against my family members, health, hope, future, calling, finances, possessions, vehicles, pets, etc."[64]

Derek Prince: "If we put on and use [the] entire protective equipment which God has provided [Eph. 6:10–18], we are totally protected from the crown of our head to the soles of our feet, except for one area. The one area for which there is no protection is our back. . . . We are not always able to protect our own back. In the legions of Rome foot soldiers fought in close ranks. . . . Every soldier knew the soldier on his right and on his left so that if he was being hard-

---

[64] Goll, *The Prophetic Intercessor*, 185–86.

pressed and could not protect his own back, there would be another soldier to do it for him. I believe the same is true with us, as Christians. We cannot go out as isolated individuals and take on the devil's kingdom."[65]

Francis Frangipane: To desire to be like Christ is a way to walk in victory. Frangipane tells us: "We cannot be successful in the heavenly war if we are not victorious in the battlefield of our minds. There is only one realm of final victory against the enemy: Christlikeness."[66]

Brother Andrew reminds us that to love those we are praying for is vital: "Remembering that we fight not against flesh and blood, but against Satan and his forces of evil, we must remind ourselves and each other constantly that every person on this planet is an object of God's love. Those who act the nastiest are that way because they have not known the love of God. Our task is the same one we talked about at the beginning of this chapter: to share the love of God with people who are hostages of Satan in a world under his control."[67]

---

[65] Derek Prince, *Spiritual Warfare* (New Kensington, PA: Whitaker House, 2001), 91–92.

[66] Francis Frangipane, *The Three Battlegrounds*, 141.

[67] Brother Andrew, *And God Changed His Mind*, with Susan DeVore Williams (Tarrytown, NY: Chosen Books, 1990), 161.

Modern-Day Examples

JOHN MULINDE—SPIRITUAL BATTLES IN UGANDA

John Mulinde, founder of World Trumpet Mission in Uganda, has faced intense spiritual warfare in his intercessory ministry for his nation. He emphasizes the importance of spiritual cleansing and maintaining a lifestyle of repentance as key strategies for protection in high-level spiritual warfare, saying:

"Repentance is key to warfare. Most of your warfare is done when you repent; it removes the enemy's legal ground, allowing God to begin to work."[68]

GEORGE OTIS JR.—SPIRITUAL MAPPING

George Otis Jr., is known for his decades-long missions work in documenting transformed communities through prayer and "spiritual mapping."[69] According to Otis, spiritual mapping is an "informed intercession" strategy that combines prayer with practical steps in studying a region and getting to know its people. In many of his books, teachings, and documentaries, he highlights the importance of right motives, humility, and unity among intercessors when engaging in territorial-

---

[68] Mulinde and Daniel, *Prayer Altars*, 271.

[69] George Otis Jr., *Informed Intercession: Transforming Your Community Through Spiritual Mapping and Strategic Prayer* (Ventura, CA: Renew, 1999).

level spiritual warfare. It is imperative that our hearts are pure and we remain humble. Purity of heart is vital.

Practical Exercises and Activations

1. **Prayer shield visualization:** As you begin intercession, visualize putting on each piece of the armor of God, declaring its purpose and protection over you.

2. **Boundary-setting exercise:** Write down clear spiritual and emotional boundaries for your intercessory ministry. Review and adjust these regularly with a trusted mentor.

3. **Intercessory prayer journal:** Keep a journal of your prayers, noting any spiritual resistance or attacks you encounter. Use this to discern patterns and adjust your protective strategies.

4. **Scripture declaration cards:** Create cards with key scriptures on protection. Declare these over yourself before and after intense prayer sessions.

5. **Self-care checklist:** Develop a personalized self-care checklist including spiritual, emotional, and physical aspects. Use this regularly to ensure you're maintaining balance.

Conclusion

As intercessors, we are called to stand in the gap, often addressing weighty matters that can invite spiritual opposition. However, we need not fear. By applying biblical principles of spiritual protection, learning from experienced intercessors, and implementing practical strategies, we can engage in deep intercession with confidence. Remember, our ultimate protection comes from our position in Christ. As we abide in Him, we can fulfill our intercessory calling with both power and safety.

CHAPTER 16

KNOW YOUR ENEMY: UNDERSTANDING PRINCIPALITIES AND POWERS

Introduction

The concept of praying against principalities and powers is crucial, yet it is often a misunderstood aspect of spiritual warfare. While the Bible clearly speaks of these spiritual forces, misconceptions about how to pray against their influence have led many believers into ineffective practices or even spiritual danger. This chapter aims to provide a biblical foundation for understanding principalities and powers, offer practical wisdom for effective prayer, and address common misunderstandings that can lead to spiritual attacks.

Biblical Foundations of Principalities and Powers

OLD TESTAMENT INSIGHTS

Angelic warfare: This passage reveals the spiritual battles occurring between the archangels Gabriel and Michael and the spiritual "princes" of earthly kingdoms.

> The prince of the Persian kingdom resisted me [Gabriel] twenty-one days. Then Michael, one of the chief princes, came to help me, because I was detained there with the king of Persia. . . . Soon I will return to fight against the prince of Persia, and when I go, the prince of Greece will come; but first I will tell you what is written in the Book of Truth. (No one supports me against them except Michael, your prince.)" (Dan. 10:12–14, 20–21)

Isaiah's vision of fallen spiritual beings: Often interpreted as referring to Satan, this passage hints at the rebellion and fall of spiritual powers.

> How you have fallen from heaven, morning star, son of the dawn! You have been cast

down to the earth, you who once laid low the
nations! You said in your heart, "I will ascend
to the heavens; I will raise my throne above
the stars of God; I will sit enthroned on the
mount of assembly, on the utmost heights of
Mount Zaphon. I will ascend above the tops
of the clouds; I will make myself like the
Most High." But you are brought down to
the realm of the dead, to the depths of the pit.
(Isa. 14:12–15)

NEW TESTAMENT TEACHINGS

Paul's description of spiritual forces: This key
verse outlines the different levels of spiritual
opposition believers face.

For our struggle is not against flesh and blood,
but against the rulers, against the authorities,
against the powers of this dark world and
against the spiritual forces of evil in the
heavenly realms. (Eph. 6:12)

Christ's victory over spiritual powers: Christ's
ultimate victory over all spiritual forces is the source
of believer's confidence in spiritual battle.

And having disarmed the powers and
authorities, he made a public spectacle of
them, triumphing over them by the cross.
(Col. 2:15)

He too shared in [our] humanity so that by his
death he might break the power of him who
holds the power of death—that is, the devil—
and free those who all their lives were held in
slavery by their fear of death. (Heb. 2:14–15)

Jesus' authority over spiritual realms: Believers'
authority in spiritual warfare is not their own, but
is derived from Christ's authority and must be
exercised in communion with Him.

Then Jesus came to them and said, "All
authority in heaven and on earth has been
given to me." (Matt. 28:18)

Jesus called his twelve disciples to him and
gave them authority to drive out impure
spirits and to heal every disease and sickness.
(Matt. 10:1)

Understanding Principalities and Powers

- **Hierarchical structure:** Scripture suggests a hierarchical structure in the spiritual realm, with various levels of authority and influence.
- **Territorial influence:** Some passages imply that certain spiritual powers have influence over geographical areas or cultural systems.
- **Limited power:** While formidable, these powers are created beings, subject to God's ultimate authority and defeated by Christ.
- **Ongoing conflict:** Despite Christ's victory, there is an ongoing spiritual conflict until the final consummation of all things.
- **Human partnership:** God calls believers to participate in this spiritual conflict through prayer and righteous living.

Common Misunderstandings and Pitfalls

- **Direct confrontation:** The misconception that believers should directly confront or name specific principalities.

- **Overemphasis:** Attributing every problem or challenge to the direct action of principalities and powers.
- **Neglecting personal responsibility:** Blaming spiritual forces for issues that may be the result of personal choices or natural circumstances.
- **Seeking special knowledge:** Attempting to gain detailed information about the spirit realm beyond what Scripture reveals.
- **Forgetting Christ's victory:** Approaching spiritual warfare from a position of fear rather than the assurance of Christ's triumph.

Biblical Approach to Praying Against Principalities and Powers

Stand in Christ's authority: Base all prayer on the finished work of Christ and His delegated authority:

He raised Christ from the dead and seated him at his right hand in the heavenly realms, far above all rule and authority, power and dominion, and every name that is invoked, not only in the present age but also in the one to come. And God placed all things under his feet and appointed him to be head over everything for the church. (Eph. 1:20–22)

Focus on God's kingdom: Emphasize the advancement of God's kingdom rather than directly addressing evil powers: "Your kingdom come, your will be done, on earth as it is in heaven" (Matt. 6:10).

The seventy-two returned with joy and said, "Lord, even the demons submit to us in your name." He replied, "I saw Satan fall like lightning from heaven. I have given you authority to trample on snakes and scorpions and to overcome all the power of the enemy; nothing will harm you. However, do not rejoice that the spirits submit to you, but rejoice that your names are written in heaven." (Luke 10:17–20)

Use Scripture: In Matthew 4, Jesus gave us the example of how to resist the temptations and attacks of the enemy through the power of the word of God. Pray the truths of Scripture, declaring God's character and promises.

For the word of God is alive and active. Sharper than any double-edged sword, it penetrates even to dividing soul and spirit, joints and marrow; it judges the thoughts and attitudes of the heart. (Heb. 4:12)

Intercede for people and situations: Focus prayer on individuals and situations affected by spiritual opposition:

I urge, then, first of all, that petitions, prayers, intercession and thanksgiving be made for all people— for kings and all those in authority, that we may live peaceful and quiet lives in all godliness and holiness. (1 Tim. 2:1–2)

Put on spiritual armor: Ephesians 6:10-18 outlines the spiritual armor of God, essential for battling against principalities and powers. This armor includes the belt of truth, breastplate of righteousness, shoes of the gospel of peace, shield of faith, helmet of salvation, and sword of the Spirit (God's word). Believers are equipped to stand firm against the schemes of the enemy, recognizing that our true battle is not against flesh and blood, but against spiritual forces of evil.

Maintain a lifestyle of holiness: Recognize that personal holiness is a key aspect of spiritual authority. As James 4:7 tells us: "Submit yourselves, then, to God. Resist the devil, and he will flee from you." Only the life of Christ in us allows us to call on the power of his name effectively.

Some Jews who went around driving out evil
spirits tried to invoke the name of the Lord
Jesus over those who were demon-possessed.
They would say, "In the name of the Jesus
whom Paul preaches, I command you to come
out." Seven sons of Sceva, a Jewish chief
priest, were doing this. One day the evil spirit
answered them, "Jesus I know, and Paul I
know about, but who are you?"
(Acts 19:13–15)

Insights from Experienced Intercessors

Cindy Jacobs: "Do not measure results by what you
see or hear. Every prayer that you pray is effective
and is like a seed planted in the ground. Continue
to water it in prayer, and it will surely produce
fruit. Keep on claiming the promise that no weapon
formed against you will prosper."[70]

C. Peter Wagner: "The personal prayer life of
one who would attempt to bind the strongman [cf.
Mark 3:27] is essential. Through prayer we draw
into intimacy with the Father so that we can most
clearly hear His voice to us. Through our personal

---

[70] Jacobs, *Possessing the Gates*, 214.

prayer lives, and also through association with other members of the Body of Christ who have gifts of intercession and prophecy and discernment of spirits, we can know what has or has not been bound in heaven [cf. Matt. 18:18]. It is foolish, as well as dangerous, to confront the enemy by binding and loosing outside the will of God or outside His timing."[71]

Modern-Day Examples

JOHN DAWSON AND CITYWIDE PRAYER INITIATIVES

John Dawson, author of *Taking Our Cities for God*, has been instrumental in organizing citywide prayer initiatives that address spiritual strongholds. He observes that an essential step in breaking the hold of sin in a city is to allow our hearts to experience the "broken heart" of God and to respond to that experience with repentance:

> Intercession is not an escape from reality. Our communication with God must be rooted in the truth—the eternal truth of His holy standards and the awful truth about our society as God sees it. The intercessor experiences the broken heart of God through the indwelling presence of the

---

[71] C. Peter Wagner, *Confronting the Powers* (Ventura, CA: Regal Books, 1996), 155.

Holy Spirit. The intercessor also identifies with the sin of the people, because the intercessor has personally contributed to God's grief. . . .

In responding to the broken heart of God, we must identify with the sins of the city in personal and corporate repentance. When Nehemiah prayed for the restoration of Jerusalem, he did not pray for the city as if he were not part of it. He said, 'I and this people have sinned' (Nehemiah 1:6-7). Through repentance, reconciliation, and prayer, the present generation can work to repair the broken-down walls of the city. . . . As you stand in the gap for your city, allow the Holy Spirit to shine the bright light of truth into the inner rooms of your soul.[72]

THE CAPTIVITY OF POTOSI

In Ana Mendez Ferrell's book *Regions of Captivity*, apostle Fernando Orihuela shares a powerful story of the glory of God coming to Potosi, an oppressed region in Bolivia. This area was rife with occultic strongholds that required years of intercession and prayer, and unifying and gathering the churches and intercessors of the region:

As we prayed over the city, past and present mixed together in images that were alive. So

---

[72] Dawson, *Taking Our Cities for God*, 143–44, 148.

much pain, so much harm had been committed against the earth and against Potosi. We could hear creation groaning to be set free. We could hear the sound of all the blood shedding linked to pain and iniquity as we earnestly interceded. Thankfully, angels came to assist us. Our prayer took a higher dimension in the spirit realm. We were able to see all the structures of evil over the city along with the horrible covenants that kept it captive. As we released the power of God over our enemy we saw chains being broken and covenants destroyed. This was an amazing experience that I could only describe as the apostle Paul said, "whether in the body or out of the body, I do not know…" (see 2 Cor. 12:3). I only know what I "saw," and it was real.

After an extended time of prayer, they started to see strongholds being broken:

After we fought along with God's angels to deliver the city, the Spirit of the Lord led us to restore the city and the land. We prayed for the blood of Christ to cover it and for the generational pain to be healed. At a certain point, the Lord led us to take Potosi out of captivity from the scary spiritual dungeons that had held it prisoner for generations.

As they continued to pray, the intercessors involved at this level became fewer in number, but their intercession became far more strategic:

> Only five people participated in this high-level warfare, which took place in three sessions. In each of them, something broke, and we saw signs in the heavens. In one of them we saw the spirit of occult over the city, it had the appearance of a huge ape who cast spells on the inhabitants to make them captives. As in the previous case, God's angels helped us break their influence, and we opened the prisons. It was beautiful to see them set free after so many years of oppression. [73]

> The results of this intercession were staggering: people began coming to Christ on their own, and in just over ten days, 40,790 precious people gave their lives to Christ!

Practical Steps for Praying Against Principalities and Powers in a Region

- **Scripture declaration:** Create a list of key scriptures about God's authority and Christ's victory. Regularly declare these in prayer.

---

[73] Ana Mendez Ferrell, *Regions of Captivity* (self-pub: Ana Mendez, 2013), 186–88.

- **Area research:** Research the history of your area, identifying historical events or patterns that might have spiritual significance.
- **Prayer mapping:** Create a spiritual map of your area, noting key institutions, cultural influences, and prayer needs.
- **United prayer:** Organize or join groups for united, focused prayer for your community or specific issues.
- **Blessing focus:** Develop a habit of regularly speaking blessings over your area, counteracting any negative spiritual influences.
- **Personal inventory:** Regularly examine your own life for areas where you might be giving ground to the enemy; maintain a lifestyle of repentance and holiness.

Conclusion

Praying against principalities and powers is a vital aspect of spiritual warfare, but it must be approached with biblical wisdom and a Christ-centered focus. By understanding the nature of these spiritual forces, avoiding common pitfalls, and adopting a biblical approach to prayer, we can effectively participate in God's work of pushing back darkness and advancing His kingdom. Remember, our ultimate victory is not in our own power or strategies, but in the finished work of Christ and our position in Him.

CHAPTER 17

WEATHER THE STORM: PRAYING THROUGH OPPOSITION AND UNEXPECTED OUTCOMES

Introduction

*I*n the journey of prophetic intercession, we will encounter challenges that test our faith and resolve. Storms of opposition, unexpected delays, and outcomes different from what we anticipated can shake our confidence and tempt us to abandon our prayer posts. This chapter explores how to maintain a steadfast prayer life in the face of adversity, drawing wisdom from biblical examples, modern-day testimonies, and practical strategies to help you persevere in your intercessory calling.

Biblical Foundations of Persevering Prayer

OLD TESTAMENT EXAMPLES

- **Elijah on Mount Carmel** (1 Kings 18:41–45): Elijah persisted in prayer for rain, sending his servant seven times to look for clouds, demonstrating perseverance in the face of apparent delay.

- **Daniel's 21-day fast** (Daniel 10:2–3, 12–14): Daniel continued in prayer and fasting for three weeks, unaware of the spiritual battle delaying his answer.

- **Nehemiah's persistent prayer** (Nehemiah 1:4–11; 2:4–5): Nehemiah prayed for months before approaching the king about rebuilding Jerusalem's walls, showing patience in waiting for God's timing.

NEW TESTAMENT EXAMPLES

- **The persistent widow** (Luke 18:1–8): Jesus taught this parable to encourage believers to pray and not give up, even when facing apparent silence or delay.

- **Paul's thorn in the flesh** (2 Corinthians 12:7–9): Three times Paul pleaded with God to remove a spiritual torment, but He replied: "My grace is sufficient for you, for my power is made perfect in weakness." Paul learned through persevering prayer to offer even his weaknesses to God.

- **Jesus in Gethsemane** (Matthew 26:36–44): Jesus prayed three times, submitting to the Father's will even when facing immense spiritual and emotional opposition.

Understanding Opposition and Unexpected Outcomes

Spiritual warfare: Ephesians 6:12 reminds us that our struggle is not against flesh and blood, but against spiritual forces of evil:

> For our struggle is not against flesh and blood, but against the rulers, against the authorities, against the powers of this dark world and against the spiritual forces of evil in the heavenly realms.

Refining of faith: James 1:2–4 teaches that trials produce perseverance and maturity in our faith:

> Consider it pure joy, my brothers and sisters, whenever you face trials of many kinds, because

you know that the testing of your faith produces perseverance. Let perseverance finish its work so that you may be mature and complete, not lacking anything.

God's higher ways: Isaiah 55:8–9 emphasizes that God's thoughts and ways are higher than ours, explaining why outcomes may differ from our expectations:

> "For my thoughts are not your thoughts, neither are your ways my ways," declares the LORD. "As the heavens are higher than the earth, so are my ways higher than your ways and my thoughts than your thoughts."

Delayed timing: 2 Peter 3:8–9 reminds us that God's timing is different from ours, and what seems like delay may be perfect divine timing:

> But do not forget this one thing, dear friends: With the LORD a day is like a thousand years, and a thousand years are like a day. The LORD is not slow in keeping his promise, as some understand slowness. Instead he is patient with you, not wanting anyone to perish, but everyone to come to repentance.

Strategies for Praying Through Opposition

1. **Stand firm in faith:** Ephesians 6:13 encourages us to put on the full armor of God to stand firm against opposition: "Therefore put on the full armor of God, so that when the day of evil comes, you may be able to stand your ground, and after you have done everything, to stand."

2. **Praise and thanksgiving:** Cultivate an attitude of gratitude even in difficult circumstances: "Give thanks in all circumstances; for this is God's will for you in Christ Jesus" (1 Thess. 5:18).

3. **Seek God's perspective:** Ask for divine wisdom and understanding of the situation: "If any of you lacks wisdom, you should ask God, who gives generously to all without finding fault, and it will be given to you" (James 1:5).

4. **Persist in prayer:** Luke 18:1 encourages us to pray and not give up: "Then Jesus told his disciples a parable to show them that they should always pray and not give up."

5. **Community support:** Seek the prayers and encouragement of fellow believers: "Carry

each other's burdens, and in this way you will fulfill the law of Christ" (Gal. 6:2).

Modern-Day Examples

REES HOWELLS AND WORLD WAR II

I have quoted from the stories of Rees Howells many times in this book because he is such a great example of a prophetic prayer warrior. During World War II, Rees Howells and his team at the Bible College of Wales faced significant opposition and unexpected turns of events. There were times when the college was plunged into darkness and apparent defeat and yet they continued interceding, sometimes for hours or even days, until they received the assurance of victory.

"Nothing was left to chance or a shot-in-the-dark type of praying. Everything was examined in God's presence and motives were sifted until the Holy Spirit could show His servant intelligently that there was an undeniable claim for prayer to be answered. Then faith would stand to the claim and lay hold of the victory; and there would be no rest until he had God's own assurance that faith had prevailed and victory was certain." [74]

---

[74] Grubb, *Rees Howells: Intercessor*, 257.

HEIDI BAKER AND MOZAMBIQUE'S TRANSFORMATION

Heidi Baker faced numerous setbacks and opposition in her ministry in Mozambique, including government resistance and natural disasters. She writes:

"We came into an atmosphere of floods, famines, and pain untold. We thought it was the perfect place to offer our lives, the perfect place to see God's kingdom established."[75]

"God's joy is our strength. We must remember this, especially when the battle gets fierce. The last eighteen months have been, by far, the most difficult of my life. Friends and babies have died; there has been sickness, floods, emotional trauma, huge financial needs, great loss of prosperity, life threats, slander, and betrayal. The more difficult it gets, however, the more tenacious we become to fix our eyes on the beautiful, perfect prize: Christ Jesus. He is always worth it all."[76]

GEORGE MÜLLER AND THE ORPHANAGES

George Müller, known for his work with orphans in Bristol, England, during the 19th century, often faced significant financial challenges. He relied solely on

---

[75] Heidi Baker, *Compelled by Love: How to Change the World Through the Simple Power of Love in Action* (Lake Mary, FL: Charisma House, 2008), 9.

[76] Baker, *Compelled by Love,* 114.

prayer to meet the needs of the orphanages, never making direct appeals for funds.[77]

Müller's unwavering faith in the face of seemingly impossible circumstances demonstrates the power of persevering prayer.

JACKIE PULLINGER AND THE WALLED CITY

Jackie Pullinger, a missionary to Hong Kong's infamous Walled City, faced intense spiritual opposition and seemingly insurmountable challenges in her work with drug addicts and gang members. In her book *Chasing The Dragon*, she shares about her persistence in prayer, despite initial lack of visible results and dangerous circumstances, and how it led to the transformation of countless lives and eventually impacted the entire community.[78]

Practical Exercises and Activations

- **Prayer mapping:** Create a visual map of your prayer situation, identifying areas of opposition or unexpected outcomes. Use this map to guide targeted prayers.

---

[77] George Müller, *Answers to Prayer, from George Müller's Narratives,* ed. A. E. C. Brooks (Chicago: Moody Press, 1985).

[78] Jackie Pullinger, *Chasing the Dragon: One Woman's Struggle Against the Darkness of Hong Kong's Drug Dens* (Grand Rapids, MI: Chosen Books, 2007).

- **Perseverance prayer journal:** Start a journal dedicated to recording your prayers, God's promises, and any progress or setbacks. Review it regularly to maintain perspective and encourage perseverance.
- **Praise break:** When facing opposition, set a timer for ten minutes and spend that time solely in praise and thanksgiving, regardless of circumstances.
- **Scripture declaration:** Choose key scriptures related to perseverance and God's faithfulness. Declare these over your situation daily.
- **Prayer partner accountability:** Find a prayer partner with whom you can share your struggles and victories. Commit to encouraging and praying for each other regularly.

Conclusion

Facing opposition, delays, and unexpected outcomes is an integral part of the intercessor's journey. By grounding ourselves in biblical truth, learning from the experiences of others, and implementing practical strategies, we can develop resilience in our prayer lives. Remember, the ultimate goal is not just to see our desired outcomes, but to grow in intimacy with God and alignment with His purposes. As we persist in prayer through every storm and setback, we become living testimonies of God's faithfulness and power.

In the words of E. M. Bounds:

> To go through the motion of praying is a dull business, though not a hard one. To say prayers in a decent, delicate way is not heavy work. But to pray really, to pray till hell feels the ponderous stroke, to pray till the iron gates of difficulty are opened, till the mountains of obstacles are removed, till the mists are exhaled and the clouds are lifted, and the sunshine of a cloudless day brightens—this is hard work, but it is God's work and man's best labor. Never was the toil of hand, head and heart less spent in vain than when praying. It is hard to wait and press and pray, and hear no voice, but stay till God answers. The joy of answered prayer is the joy of a travailing mother when a man child is born into the world, the joy of a slave whose chains have been burst asunder and to whom new life and liberty have just come.[79]

---

[79] Bounds, *The Complete Works*, 338.

CHAPTER 18

PROPHETIC ALERTS: NAVIGATING PROPHETIC WARNINGS WITH DISCERNMENT AND ACTION

Introduction

*P*rophetic warnings are a significant aspect of the prophetic intercession, and can serve as divine alerts to potential dangers or coming events. However, receiving and handling these warnings requires wisdom, discernment, and a solid biblical foundation. This chapter explores how to recognize, interpret, and respond to prophetic warnings, emphasizing the crucial role of prayer and the importance of distinguishing between genuine divine insights and personal opinions

Biblical Foundations of Prophetic Warnings

OLD TESTAMENT EXAMPLES

- **Noah and the flood** (Genesis 6:13–14): "So God said to Noah, 'I am going to put an end to all people, for the earth is filled with violence because of them. I am surely going to destroy both them and the earth. So make yourself an ark of cypress wood; make rooms in it and coat it with pitch inside and out.'"

- **Joseph's interpretation of Pharaoh's dream** (Genesis 41:25–32): "Then Joseph said to Pharaoh, 'The dreams of Pharaoh are one and the same. God has revealed to Pharaoh what he is about to do. The seven good cows are seven years, and the seven good heads of grain are seven years; it is one and the same dream. The seven lean, ugly cows that came up afterward are seven years, and so are the seven worthless heads of grain scorched by the east wind: They are seven years of famine'" (vv. 25–27).

- **Jonah's warning to Nineveh** (Jonah 3:4–5): "Jonah began by going a day's journey into the city, proclaiming, 'Forty more days and Nineveh will be overthrown.' The Ninevites believed God. A fast was proclaimed, and all of them, from the greatest to the least, put on sackcloth."

NEW TESTAMENT TEACHINGS

- **Jesus' warnings about the future** (Matthew 24:4–5): "Watch out that no one deceives you. For many will come in my name, claiming, 'I am the Messiah,' and will deceive many."

- **Paul's warning to the Ephesian elders** (Acts 20:28–31): "Keep watch over yourselves and all the flock of which the Holy Spirit has made you overseers. Be shepherds of the church of God, which he bought with his own blood. I know that after I leave, savage wolves will come in among you and will not spare the flock. Even from your own number men will arise and distort the truth in order to draw away disciples after them. So be on your guard!"

Understanding Prophetic Warnings

Purpose of warnings: Prophetic warnings are not merely to inform but primarily to prompt prayer and, when appropriate, action.

God's heart in warnings: Warnings reflect God's love and desire to protect and prepare His people.

Conditional nature: Many prophetic warnings are conditional, dependent on people's response (e.g., Jonah and Nineveh).

Timing considerations: Warnings may be for immediate, near future, or distant future events.

Personal vs. corporate: Warnings can be for individuals, communities, nations, or the global church.

Discerning Genuine Prophetic Warnings

1. **Alignment with Scripture:** Genuine warnings will never contradict God's written Word: "All Scripture is God-breathed and is useful for teaching, rebuking, correcting and training in righteousness, so that the servant of God may be thoroughly equipped for every good work" (2 Tim. 3:16–17).

2. **Confirmation:** Seek confirmation through prayer, wise counsel, and multiple trusted prophetic voices: "For lack of guidance a nation falls, but victory is won through many advisers" (Prov. 11:14).

3. **Fruit of the Spirit:** True prophetic warnings, even when sobering, should ultimately produce

the fruit of the Spirit: "The fruit of the Spirit is love, joy, peace, forbearance, kindness, goodness, faithfulness, gentleness and self-control. Against such things there is no law" (Gal. 5:22–23).

4. **Inner witness of the Holy Spirit:** Learn to discern the inner confirmation of the Holy Spirit: "Dear friends, do not believe every spirit, but test the spirits to see whether they are from God, because many false prophets have gone out into the world" (1 John 4:1).

5. **Humility:** True prophetic warnings are often delivered with humility, not arrogance or self-promotion, or glee that people are going to "learn their lesson." James tells us that "God opposes the proud but shows favor to the humble" and advises: "Humble yourselves before the Lord, and he will lift you up" (James 4:6, 10).

Responding to Prophetic Warnings

- **Prayer:** The primary response to a prophetic warning should be intensified, focused prayer.
- **Seek wisdom:** Ask God for wisdom on how to interpret and respond to the warning.

- **Repentance:** If applicable, respond with repentance and course correction.
- **Preparation:** Take practical steps of preparation as led by the Holy Spirit.
- **Sharing:** Carefully consider if and how to share the warning with others, always led by wisdom and love.

Insights from Experienced Prophetic Voices

Rick Joyner: "I have had a number of prophetic warnings that were very useful, and I think they have saved us from serious setbacks. However, I am very wary of any warning that I am given with a spirit of fear attached to it."[80]

Cindy Jacobs: "We may sense danger or feel great sorrow when we think about another person. This is the Holy Spirit's prompting within us. It is at this moment that we stand in the gap, and the heart of God is expressed in intercession. God then begins to move on behalf of the one for whom we have prayed; His Kingdom has come into that person's life, and His will is done."[81]

---

[80] Rick Joyner, *The Prophetic Ministry* (New Kensington, PA: Whitaker House, 2006), 116.

[81] Jacobs, *Possessing the Gates*, 64.

Examples of Fulfilled Prophetic Warnings

JOHN PAUL JACKSON'S "PERFECT STORM" PROPHECY

In 2008, John Paul Jackson prophesied about a coming "perfect storm" of simultaneous crises in various sectors including economics, government, religious structures, and weather patterns.[82]

Actions Taken:

- Jackson taught extensively on preparation, both spiritual and practical.
- He encouraged believers to deepen their faith and become sources of stability in their communities.

Outcome: Many aspects of this prophecy have been seen as fulfilled in events such as the 2008 financial crisis, political upheavals, and increasing natural disasters.

JOSHUA GILES' PROPHECY OF A GLOBAL PANDEMIC

In December 2019, Joshua Giles, author, pastor and prophet, shared a warning about a coming pandemic in his book *Prophetic Forecast*, Giles wrote, "When I was given a prophetic word in 2015 to prepare for

---

[82] John Paul Jackson, "The Coming Perfect Storm," *Stream Ministries,* December 19, 2008, https://www.youtube.com/watch?v=kzPJjOzZorg.

2020 and the new era that we would enter, I was a little shocked at what I heard and saw. At that time, the Lord spoke to me of a virus that would mimic other diseases, and I saw it in a lab in a vision. God said that it would be a strain we had never seen. I shared this with my church that year in a prophetic service, and many of the members recorded the prophecy. Then in 2019, the Lord showed me in a vision people wearing masks. In this vision, people in airports and all kinds of places had masks on. I was stunned because there was no talk of a pandemic at that time. The Lord warns us of things to come, however, that we might not be caught off guard. Through the years, I have learned that when God speaks it or shows it, we need to respond by praying about it and preparing."[83]

Actions Taken:

- Giles urged believers to pray for protection and divine intervention.
- He encouraged people to take practical steps for health and safety.

Outcome: The COVID-19 pandemic began spreading globally in early 2020, affecting millions worldwide.

---

[83] Joshua Giles, *Prophetic Forecast: Insights for Navigating the Future to Align with Heaven's Agenda* (Shippensburg, PA: Destiny Image Publishers, 2019), Kindle location 198–199 of 240.

Giles later comments:

> This new era will be filled with conflict
> and wars. It is important that you remain
> grounded in the Lord and keep a sound mind.
> Remember, 2 Timothy 1:7 says, "For God
> has not given us a spirit of fear, but of power
> and of love and of a sound mind." God's
> immeasurable, unfailing love will be your
> comfort, and the power of the Holy Spirit
> will sustain you. So it is imperative that you
> guard your ear gates and your eye gates from
> anything that is contrary to the Word of God.
> Your ears and eyes are the gateway to your
> emotions, to your thinking and ultimately
> to your soul. Amid mounting warfare, you
> will have the peace of God that passes all
> understanding (see Philippians 4:6–7).[84]

Practical Steps for Handling Prophetic Warnings

- **Prayer journal:** Keep a journal of prophetic warnings received, including your prayers and any confirmations or outcomes.

---

[84] Giles, *Prophetic Forecast*, Kindle location 225 of 240.

- **Accountability partner:** Establish a relationship with a mature believer who can help you process and discern prophetic warnings.
- **Scripture study:** Regularly study biblical examples of prophetic warnings and their outcomes to sharpen your discernment.
- **Fasting for clarity:** Consider fasting when seeking clarity on a significant prophetic warning.
- **Prophetic intercession groups:** Join or form a group dedicated to praying through prophetic insights and warnings.

Conclusion

Prophetic warnings are a vital part of God's communication with His people, serving to protect, prepare, and position us for His purposes. The key to handling these warnings effectively lies in maintaining a biblical perspective, exercising careful discernment, and responding primarily through prayer and intercession. As we grow in our ability to recognize and respond to genuine prophetic warnings, we partner more closely with God's heart for individuals, communities, and nations. Remember, the ultimate goal of prophetic ministry, including warnings, is to draw people closer to God and align them with His redemptive purposes.

Part V

CHARTING YOUR COURSE: PRACTICAL APPLICATION AND RESOURCES

CHAPTER 19

MAPPING THE JOURNEY: A STRATEGIC GUIDE FOR YOUR PRAYER TIME

*W*hether you're new to the idea of prophetic intercession or seeking to deepen your existing prayer life, this chapter offers a guide to help you navigate how to pray. Think of this chapter like a map that helps you explore the steps and practices of prophetic intercession. However, remember that this is a tool, not a rigid set of rules. I call it a map because it provides direction and landmarks, but the specific path you take may vary. Your relationship with God is unique, and your practice of prophetic intercession will be equally personal.

This "map" is designed to offer structure for beginners and inspiration for those more experienced. It's a starting point, a framework to build upon as you develop your own style of prophetic intercession. As you read, remain open to the Holy Spirit's guidance, allowing these suggestions to enhance, not constrain, your prayer life. As one of my students once said: "Tools aren't rules"!

Below you will find twelve steps that can help you enter into God's presence, listen for His voice, and intercede effectively for others. Remember, the goal is not perfection but connection—deepening your relationship with God and becoming a channel of His love and wisdom in the world.

1. Enter God's Presence

Begin your journey by intentionally entering God's presence. Create a quiet, distraction-free environment where you can focus on God.

Enter his gates with thanksgiving and his courts with praise; give thanks to him and praise his name. (Ps. 100:4)

Practice: Start with a time of worship or contemplative prayer. Focus on God's attributes and express your gratitude.

Reflection Questions:

- How do you typically prepare yourself to enter God's presence?
- What distractions do you often face, and how can you minimize them?
- Describe a time when you felt particularly close to God. What contributed to that experience?

2. Listen for God's Voice

Cultivate an attitude of attentiveness, waiting on God to speak. Remember, God can communicate in various ways—through thoughts, impressions, scriptures, dreams, or visions, to name a few.

"My sheep listen to my voice; I know them, and they follow me." (John 10:27)

Practice: Spend time in silence, focusing on God. Write down any thoughts, impressions, or scriptures that come to mind.

Listening to God is essential to walking with God.—Charles Stanley[85]

---

[85] Charles Stanley, "Listening to God and Walking with God," *Sermons.love,* accessed September 12, 2024, https://sermons.love/charles-stanley/3917-charles-stanley-listening-to-god-and-walking-with-god.html.

Reflection Questions

- In what ways have you experienced God speaking to you in the past?
- How do you distinguish between God's voice and your own thoughts?
- What practices help you to quiet your mind and listen more effectively?

3. Discern the Message

Learn to differentiate between personal messages and those intended for intercession. Test all impressions against Scripture and seek confirmation.

Dear friends, do not believe every spirit, but test the spirits to see whether they are from God. (1 John 4:1)

Practice: For each impression, ask: Does this align with Scripture? Is it for me or for others? Seek wisdom from mature believers if unsure.

Discernment is not knowing the difference between right and wrong. It is knowing the difference between right and almost right.
—Charles Spurgeon[86]

---

[86] This quotation is popularly attributed to Charles Spurgeon, *Apologetics315,* https://apologetics315.com/2013/02/charles-spurgeon-on-discernment/.

Reflection Questions

- What criteria do you use to test whether a message is from God?
- Can you recall a time when you received a message that wasn't for you personally? How did you know?

4. Reflect and Apply (if personal)

If the message is personal, take time to reflect on its meaning and how to apply it to your life.

Do not merely listen to the word, and so deceive yourselves. Do what it says.
(James 1:22)

Practice: Journal about the personal message. What does it mean for your life? What actions can you take in response?

Reflection Questions

- How do you typically respond to personal messages from God?
- What challenges do you face in applying God's personal messages to your life?
- Describe a time when applying a personal message from God led to significant growth or change in your life.

5. Intercede (if for others)

To pray effectively for others, align with God's will and pray with compassion.

I urge, then, first of all, that petitions, prayers, intercession and thanksgiving be made for all people. (1 Tim. 2:1)

Practice: Pray specifically for the person or situation God has brought to mind. Ask for God's will to be done and for His love to be manifest.

God does nothing but by prayer, and everything with it. —John Wesley[87]

Reflection Questions:

- How does your approach to prayer change when interceding for others compared to praying for yourself?
- What emotions do you experience when interceding for others?

---

[87] Excerpts from John Wesley posted on *The Jesus Gathering,* accessed September 12, 2024, https://www.thejesusgathering.org/john-wesley.html. The full quotation is: "God does nothing but in answer to prayer; and even they who have been converted to God without praying for it themselves, (which is exceeding rare,) were not without the prayers of others. Every new victory which a soul gains is the effect of a new prayer." John Wesley, *A Plain Account of Christian Perfection* (Boston: McDonald Gill & Co., 1880), 98.

- How do you maintain focus and energy during extended periods of intercession?

6. Declare God's Will

Learn to make faith-filled declarations based on the insights received, speaking God's truth over situations.

You will also declare a thing, and it will be established for you; so light will shine on your ways. (Job 22:28, NKJV)

Practice: Formulate declarations based on your prayers. For example, "In Jesus' name, I declare healing over [person's name]."

Reflection Questions:

- What does it mean to you to "declare God's will"?
- How comfortable are you with making faith-filled declarations? Why?
- Can you share an experience where declaring God's will led to a noticeable change in a situation?

7. Wait on God

After initial intercession, maintain a posture of patience and continued listening.

Wait for the LORD; be strong and take heart
and wait for the LORD. (Ps. 27:14)

Practice: Spend time in silent expectation after your declarations. Be open to further insights or direction from God.

Reflection Questions:

- What does "waiting on God" look like in your personal practice?

- How do you maintain patience and attentiveness during times of waiting?

- Can you describe a time when waiting on God resulted in a deeper understanding or breakthrough?

8. Discern Further Guidance

Learn to recognize whether God has more to reveal or if the session is complete.

Whether you turn to the right or to the left,
your ears will hear a voice behind you,
saying, "This is the way; walk in it."
(Isa. 30:21)

Practice: Ask God if there's more He wants to reveal. Be sensitive to a sense of completion or further promptings.

Reflection Questions:

- How do you recognize when God has more to reveal versus when a prayer session is complete?
- What signs or feelings do you experience when you sense God is providing further guidance?
- How do you balance being open to more guidance with the need to conclude a prayer session?

9. Give Thanks and Praise

Regardless of the outcome, cultivate an attitude of gratitude and worship.

Give thanks in all circumstances; for this is
God's will for you in Christ Jesus.
(1 Thess. 5:18)

Practice: Spend time thanking God for His presence, guidance, and work in the situation you've prayed about.

Reflection Questions:

- How does incorporating thanksgiving and praise impact your prayer life?
- In what ways do you express gratitude and worship after a prayer session?
- How do you maintain an attitude of thankfulness even when you don't see immediate results from your prayers?

10. Act on Guidance

Consider practical steps you can take in response to the intercession.

Faith by itself, if it is not accompanied by action, is dead. (James 2:17)

Practice: Reflect on any actions God might be prompting you to take. This could involve encouraging someone, offering practical help, or continuing in prayer.

Reflection Questions:

- What steps do you typically take to act on the guidance you receive during prayer?
- Can you share an example of a time when acting on guidance from prayer led to a significant outcome?

- How do you discern between actions you should take and matters you should continue to pray about?

11. Record and Share

Document your experience and, when appropriate, share your insights with others.

"Write down the revelation and make it plain on tablets so that a herald may run with it." (Hab. 2:2)

Practice: Keep a prayer journal to record your experiences. When sharing with others, do so with humility and wisdom.

Reflection Questions:

- What methods do you use to record your prayer experiences and insights?
- How do you decide what to share with others and what to keep private?
- In what ways has sharing your prophetic insights impacted others or yourself?

12. Evaluate and Learn

Reflect on your experience to grow in your prophetic gifting and prophetic intercession.

Test everything. Hold on to the good.
(1 Thess. 5:21, EHV)

Practice: Ask yourself: What did I learn about God? About myself? How can I grow from this experience?

Reflection Questions:

- How often do you take time to reflect on and evaluate your prayer experiences?
- What have been some of the most significant lessons you've learned through your practice of prophetic intercession?
- How has your approach to prophetic intercession changed over time, and what prompted these changes?

Conclusion

Remember, prophetic intercession is a journey that you will grow into. Be patient with yourself and always remain humble and teachable. As you practice these steps, you'll grow in your ability to partner with God in prayer and prophecy.

The prayer of a righteous person is powerful
and effective. (James 5:16)

The twelve steps discussed in this chapter—from entering God's presence to evaluating and learning from your experiences—provide a framework, but they are not a rigid formula. As you grow in your practice of prophetic intercession, you may find that some steps naturally flow together, while others may require more focus depending on the situation.

THE JOURNEY CONTINUES

Thank you for taking the time to read this guide on prophetic intercession. Remember, the heart of prophetic intercession is not about following a set of rules, but about cultivating a deep, listening relationship with God. It's about being willing to be used as a vessel for His love and wisdom in the world. Sometimes, this might mean spending an extended time in silent listening. Other times, it might involve bold declarations or fervent prayers for others.

As you continue on this journey, be patient with yourself. There may be times when you feel deeply connected and other times when you feel unsure. Both are normal parts of the process. The key is to remain faithful in showing up, opening your heart, and being willing to partner with God.

Don't be afraid to adjust your approach as you learn what works best for you. Some may find journaling helpful, while others might prefer verbal prayer. Some might be drawn to long periods of silent contemplation, while others might engage in more active forms of prayer. All of these can be valid expressions of prophetic intercession.

Finally, remember that prophetic intercession is not just about the moments of prayer, but about cultivating a lifestyle of sensitivity to God's voice and compassion for others. As you practice these steps, you may find that your entire perspective on life begins to shift, seeing the world more and more through God's eyes of love.

May this guide serve as a helpful companion on your journey of prophetic intercession. As you continue to grow in this practice, may you experience the joy of partnering with God in bringing His kingdom to earth, one prayer at a time!

BIBLIOGRAPHY

Alves, Elizabeth. *Becoming a Prayer Warrior: A Guide to Effective and Powerful Prayer*. Minneapolis: Chosen Books, 2016.

Baker, Heidi. *Compelled by Love: How to Change the World Through the Simple Power of Love in Action*. With Shara Pradhan. Lake Mary, FL: Charisma House, 2008.

———. "Fasting," Facebook, September 6, 2019. https://www.facebook.com/photo.php?fbid=2630797913610570&id=170111516345901&set=a.498038696886513.

Baker, Heidi, and Jennifer Miscov. "Jesus Said, 'Come into the Desert with Me.'" *Destiny Image*. Accessed September 20, 2024, https://www.destinyimage.com/blog/heidi-baker-jennifer-miskov-come-into-the-desert-with-me.

Bounds, E. M. *The Complete Works of E. M. Bounds on Prayer: Experience the Wonders of God through Prayer*. Grand Rapids, MI: Baker Books, 1990.

Brother Andrew. *And God Changed His Mind*. With Susan DeVore Williams. Tarrytown, NY: Chosen Books, 1990.

Catherine of Siena. *The Letters of Catherine of Siena.* Translated by Suzanne Noffke. Tempe, AZ: Arizona Center for Medieval and Renaissance Studies, 2000.

Cauchi, Tony. "Evans Roberts and War on the Saints." *Sermonindex.* November 2007. https://www.sermonindex. net/modules/newbb/viewtopic.php?topic_id=32414&forum=40.

Chavda, Mahesh. *The Hidden Power of Speaking in Tongues.* Shippensburg, PA: Destiny Image Publishers, 2003.

Dawson, John. *Taking Our Cities for God.* Lake Mary, FL: Charisma House, 2001.

Elsheimer, Janice. *The Creative Call: An Artist's Response to the Way of the Spirit.* Colorado Springs: WaterBrook Press, 2001.

Engle, Lou, and Dean Briggs. *The Jesus Fast: The Call to Awaken the Nations.* Minneapolis: Chosen Books, 2016.

Ernst, Manfred, ed. *Globalization and the Re-shaping of Christianity in the Pacific Islands.* Suva: Pacific Theological College, 2006.

Ferrell, Ana Mendez. *Regions of Captivity.* Self-published: Ana Mendez, 2013.

Fischer, Klaus. *Nazi Germany: A New History.* New York: Continuum, 1995.

Fox, George. *The Journal of George Fox.* Edited by John L. Nickalls. Philadelphia: Philadelphia Yearly Meeting of the Religious Society of Friends, 1997.

Frangipane, Francis. *The Three Battlegrounds: The Mind, the Church & the Heavenly Places.* Chichester, UK: New Wine Press, 1994.

Fuhrer, Christian. "Voices of a Revolution: Leipzig." NPR, November 9, 2009. https://www.npr.org/2009/11/09/120251039/voices-of-a-revolution-leipzig.

Giles, Joshua. *Prophetic Forecast: Insights for Navigating the Future to Align with Heaven's Agenda.* Shippensburg, PA: Destiny Image Publishers, 2019.

Godwin, Roy, and Dave Roberts. *The Grace Outpouring: Becoming a People of Blessing.* Colorado Springs: David C. Cook, 2012.

Goll, James W. *The Prophetic Intercessor: Releasing God's Purposes to Change Lives and Influence Nations.* Grand Rapids, MI: Chosen Books, 2007.

Green, Josh. "The Call to Desperate Intercession: What is Travailing Prayer?" *24-7 Prayer.* Accessed September 20, 2024. https://www.24-7prayer.com/the-call-to-desperate-intercession-what-is-travailing-prayer/.

Grubb, Norman P. *Rees Howells: Intercessor.* Fort Washington, PA: Christian Literature Crusade, 1952.

Hagin, Kenneth. *Tongues—Beyond the Upper Room.* Broken Arrow, OK: RHEMA Bible Church, 2007.

Hildegard of Bingen. *Scivias.* Translated by Mother Columba Hart and Jane Bishop. Mahwah, NJ: Paulist Press, 1990.

"Hill of Slane; The Coming of Christianity." Accessed September 30, 2024. https://www.discoverboynevalley. ie/boyne-valley-drive/heritage-sites/hill-slane-coming-christianity.

Holden, Constance. "Tongues on the Mind." *Science.* November 2, 2006. https://www.science.org/content/article/ tongues-mind.

Jackson, John Paul. "The Coming Perfect Storm." *Stream Ministries.* December 19, 2008. https://www.youtube.com/ watch?v=kzPJjOzZorg.

Jacobs, Cindy. *Possessing the Gates of the Enemy: A Training Manual for Militant Intercession.* Grand Rapids, MI: Chosen Books, 1991.

———. *The Prophetic Ministry.* New Kensington, PA: Whitaker House, 2006.

———. "Your Prayers are Weapons Shaping History in Times of War." YouTube, November 19, 2023. https:// youtu.be/VqRU6S9OC_g?si=Lenj3EudZLdUPG_N.

Joyner, Rick. *The Final Quest.* Fort Mill, SC: Morningstar Publications, 1997.

L'Engle, Madeleine. *Walking on Water: Reflections on Faith and Art.* New York: Convergent Books, 2016.

Lockett, Matt. "Rees Howells: How Prayers Played a Role in Ending Hitler's Reign of Death." *Justice House of Prayer DC.* Accessed September 20, 2024. https://www. jhopdc.com/rees-howells-part-2.

Mandryk, Jason. *Operation World: The Definitive Prayer Guide to Every Nation.* 7th ed. Crown Hill, UK: Authentic Media, 2010.

Meyer, Julie. *Singing the Scriptures: How All Believers Can Experience Breakthrough, Hope and Healing.* Minneapolis: Chosen Books, 2018.

Moore, Beth. "It's Prayer. That's the Thing." *Living Proof Ministries.* February 4, 2015. https://blog.lproof. org/2015/02/its-prayer-thats-the-thing.html.

Mulinde, John, and Mark Daniel. *Prayer Altars: A Strategy That Is Changing Nations.* Lake Mary, FL: Creation House, 2013.

Müller, George. *Answers to Prayer, from George Müller's Narratives.* Edited by A. E. C. Brooks. Chicago: Moody Press, 1985.

Najapfour, Brian G. "'Give me Scotland, or I die'" John Knox as a Man of Prayer." *The Heritage Blog.* Accessed September 12, 2024. https://www.theheritage.blog/knox-man-of-prayer.

Otis, George, Jr. "George Otis and Transformational Revival." Interview by Tim Fellows. *Love Black Country,* September 2020. https://www.youtube.com/watch?v=ROgi5o1V7XY.

———. *Informed Intercession: Transforming Your Community Through Spiritual Mapping and Strategic Prayer.* Ventura, CA: Renew, 1999.

————. "Snapshots of Glory." *Renewal Journal* *17* (September 12, 2011). https://renewaljournal. com/2011/09/12/snapshots-of-glory-bygeorge-otis-jr/.

————. *Transformations: A Documentary.* New York: The Sentinel Group, 1999. DVD.

Pierce, Chuck D. *The Future War of the Church.* Ventura, CA: Regal Books, 2001.

Pollock, Dennis. "Evan Roberts & the Welsh Revival." *Spirit of Grace Ministries.* Accessed September 12, 2024. https://www.spiritofgrace.org/articles/nl_2014/extras/00_ evan_roberts.html.

Prince, Derek. *Spiritual Warfare.* New Kensington, PA: Whitaker House, 2001.

Pullinger, Jackie. *Chasing the Dragon: One Woman's Struggle Against the Darkness of Hong Kong's Drug Dens.* Grand Rapids, MI: Chosen Books, 2007.

Ravenhill, Leonard. *Why Revival Tarries.* Minneapolis: Bethany House Publishers, 1987.

Roberts, Evan. "Keys for Revival." *The Revival Library.* Accessed September 12, 2024. https://revival-library.org/ revival-resources/for-revival-seekers/revival-tips-from-history/evan-roberts-keys-of-revival/.

Ruscoe, Doris M. *The Intercession of Rees Howells, 1879–1950.* Fort Washington, PA: Christian Literature Crusade, 1983.

Sithole, Surprise. *Voice in the Night: The True Story of the Man and Miracles That Are Changing Africa.* Grand Rapids, MI: Chosen Books, 2012.

Spurgeon, Charles. *Apologetics315.* Accessed September 12, 2024. https://apologetics315.com/2013/02/charles-spurgeon-on-discernment/.

Stanley, Charles. "Listening to God and Walking with God." *Sermons.love.* Accessed September 12, 2024. https://sermons.love/charles-stanley/3917-charles-stanley-listening-to-god-and-walking-with-god.html.

Stead, W. T. "Evan Roberts." In *The Welsh Revival*, edited by W. T. Stead and G. Campbell Morgan, 48–63. Boston: The Pilgrim Press, 1905.

Sutton, Richard. "Ffald-y-Brenin – A Place of Blessing." *A Listening Heart.* Accessed September 12, 2024. https://alisteningheart.blog/2018/08/01/ffald-y-brenin-a-place-of-blessing/.

Swearingen, Chet and Phyllis Swearingen. "1995 Cali, Colombia Revival." *Beautiful Feet.* Accessed September 12, 2024. https://romans1015.com/cali/.

Tertullian. *A Treatise on the Soul.* In *Ante-Nicene Fathers.* Vol. 3, *Latin Christianity,* edited by Alexander Roberts and James Donaldson, 181–235. New York, Christian Literature Publishing, 1885.

Van Natta, Bruce. "Bruce Van Natta: Saved by Angels." Interview with *CBN.* October 12, 2022. https://cbn.com/article/not-selected/bruce-van-natta-saved-angels.

Wagner, Peter C. *Breaking Spiritual Strongholds in Your City.* Shippensburg, PA: Destiny Image Publishers, 1993.

————. *Confronting the Powers.* Ventura, CA: Regal Books, 1996.

Wesley, John. *A Plain Account of Christian Perfection.* Boston: McDonald Gill & Co., 1880.

Yeager, Michael. *Travailing in Prayer: Understanding Intercessory Prayer.* Self-published: Michael H. Yeager, 2023.

Z, Joseph. *Servants of Fire.* Shippensburg, PA: Harrison House, 2023.

ABOUT THE AUTHOR

*R*oma Waterman is the founder of HeartSong Prophetic Alliance, a thriving online training school that teaches thousands of students worldwide. She is a prophetic voice, worship leader/singer, songwriter and author and is passionate about raising prophetic communities that influence all spheres of society.

As a first-generation Australian, Roma was heavily influenced by her Italian immigrant parents and grandparents. She would often listen to her grandfather play the piano and sing songs of his motherland with love and conviction. In addition to this connection to her heritage, she was also influenced by her time growing up in the church. She not only saw lives transformed, but creative miracles, signs, and wonders were a normal part of her church experience. Her desire to grow closer to God grew daily, along with her love for music.

What she did with those passions has shaped her life and the lives of so many others.

The founder of The Melbourne Gospel choir, she has served as a session vocalist for many television shows as well as a vocal coach for The Voice, The X Factor and Australian Idol. She has recorded many albums and won several international songwriting awards, including The Gospel Music Associations Honour award for outstanding contribution to Christian music, and the 2020 Legacy Award in recognition of outstanding contribution and service to media and the arts.

While these roles have all been incredible for Roma's passion in raising up others, her most prized title has been Mom. However, getting to this place has not been easy. During her early 20s, Roma struggled with endometriosis and fibromyalgia. These painful experiences almost stopped her from being in ministry. Miraculously, she was totally healed. She loves to declare the goodness of God when she speaks of the miraculous conception and birth of her two beautiful kids, Angel and Asa, and loves to pray for others who struggle in this area, where she has seen many healings take place in the lives of others.

Her passion for being a prophetic voice has led her across the globe as a minister, teacher, and trainer, with the prophetic and miraculous being a mark of her ministry. Her passion is to help others receive supernatural blueprints for their lives and she loves to train and raise up others.

Roma holds a Graduate Diploma of Theology and loves teaching on the contemplative practices, Christian meditation and prayer from a prophetic viewpoint. Along with her husband, Ted, they reside in Melbourne, Australia, with their two children and are a part of the leadership in their thriving local church which is currently experiencing a remarkable outpouring of the Lord's manifest presence.

To Find out more about Roma:

Website: www.romawaterman.com

Online Training: www.training.romawaterman.com

Books: https://www.amazon.com/author/romawaterman

Printed in the USA
CPSIA information can be obtained
at www.ICGtesting.com
LVHW021115051124
795747LV00014B/674